COSPLAY

THE FANTASY WORLD OF ROLE PLAY

THIS IS A CARLTON BOOK

Published in 2015 by Carlton Books Limited
20 Mortimer Street
London W1T 3JW

Text © Carlton Books Ltd, 2015
Design © Carlton Books Ltd, 2015

A CIP catalogue record for this book is
available from the British Library.

ISBN 978 1 78097 630 3

Printed in China

COSPLAY

THE FANTASY WORLD OF ROLE PLAY

LAUREN ORSINI

CARLTON
BOOKS

CONTENTS

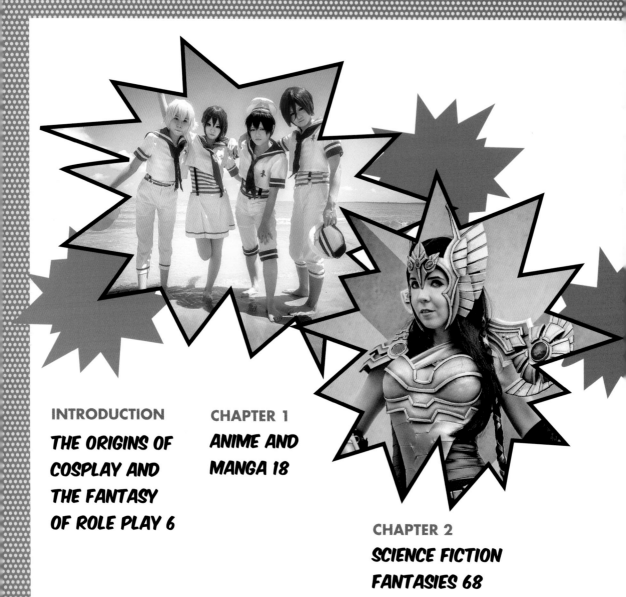

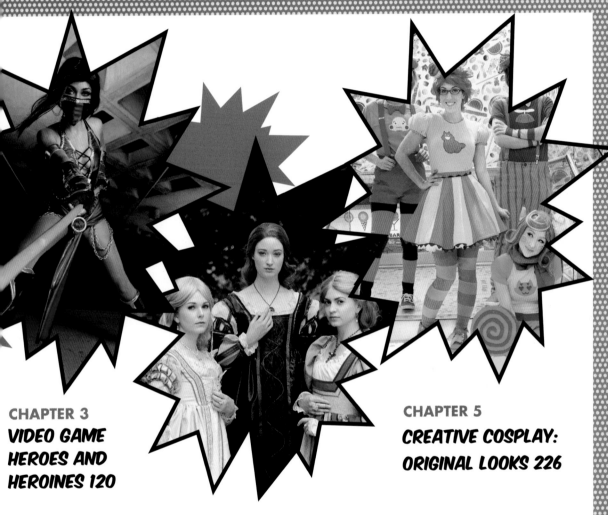

INTRODUCTION: THE ORIGINS OF COSPLAY AND THE FANTASY OF ROLE PLAY

SOMETIMES COSPLAYERS COMBINE
ELEMENTS OF DIFFERENT CHARACTERS
TO HUMOROUS EFFECT. HERE TWO ANGRY
BIRD TRANSFORMERS WEAR THE AUTOBOT
ARMOUR OF OPTIMUS PRIME AND ARCEE,
AND HAVE THE FACES OF BIRDS FROM THE
POPULAR GAME. PHOTOGRAPHED AT NEW
YORK COMIC CON BY MICHAEL STEWART.

In bright colours and outlandish styles, they don't look as if they're from this world. But here they are, posing at fan conventions, competing in costume contests or shooting pictures at the local park. These people are cosplayers, people who dedicate hours to selecting, organizing, constructing and getting in character for elaborate fantasy outfits.

Sometimes you can recognize a cosplayer's costume as emulating a character from a film, television show or book. But not always: some cosplays are custom designs inspired by a fictional place or time far in the past or future, or even fantasy personas – like fairies, cyberpunks or even real or mythical animals.

"I view cosplaying as showing an appreciation of some aspect of a character," says cosplayer Adam Burakowski, who also goes by the name of Dr_Teng, "whether that be a visually appealing design, personality or the emotional meaning the character may hold for the person cosplaying."

Cosplay encompasses a wide genre of costuming styles, which can be a hurdle for anyone attempting to describe this creative hobby. Generally, cosplay is defined as the art and craft of assuming both the appearance and persona of a fictional character. What differentiates cosplay and dressing-up is that cosplayers take on a theatrical persona while in costume.

Cosplayers swan across the convention floor, posing and speaking almost like the character you recognize. However, be aware that this is a very intentional act. It's less about playing make-believe than about creating an illusion for fellow fans.

As cosplayer Renee Michelle puts it, "It feels a bit weird whenever I read/hear about cosplay in the media these days, because I'm still not used to other people knowing what it is. However, I always cringe whenever the media describes cosplay as 'not just dressing up, but pretending that you're the character'. I would strongly disagree – while there are definitely people who are drawn to cosplay solely because they want to embody a character about whom they're passionate, you can also make costumes because you love the design, because you love the source material, and/or you want to challenge yourself or learn a new technique. Or maybe you just want to hang out with friends."

In fact, a desire to hang out with and impress some friends is exactly how cosplay began. Cosplay dates back to 1939, when two science-fiction fans unintentionally invented it. The scene was the very first World Science Fiction Convention in New York City, a somewhat sedate gathering of science-fiction artists, writers and fans to debate their theories about the genre of science fiction.

Suddenly, in walked 22-year-old Forrest J. Ackerman and Myrtle R. Jones, and the sombre mood broke. The two fans were dressed in styles from the twenty-fifth century: Ackerman as a space explorer, Jones in a gown inspired by the 1936 sci-fi film *Things To Come*. Jones crafted both costumes herself. The costumes added an air of the absurd to the event, perhaps inspiring the ebullient gatherings of today's conventions and avoiding the dry academic conferences they might have otherwise become.

It wasn't just their costumes that made a splash. Ackerman was in character too. He greeted other attendees in Esperanto, informing them he was a traveller from the

ABOVE LEFT A PROGRAMME FROM THE 1939 WORLD SCIENCE FICTION CONVENTION, THE BIRTHPLACE OF COSPLAY.

ABOVE RIGHT FORREST J. ACKERMAN AND MYRTLE R. JONES IN THEIR FUTURISTIC WORLDCON FINERY.

BELOW THE FIRST APPEARANCE OF THE WORD "COSPLAY", IN TAKAHASHI NOBUYUKI'S 1984 WRITEUP OF LOS ANGELES WORLDCON.

future. They were the only people dressed in "futuristicostume" that year, but the practice soon caught on. Just a year later, in 1940, a few dozen fans showed up in hand-crafted outfits of their own.

Ackerman, who later became a fandom convention reporter, saw firsthand the chaos he had unleashed. Seventeen years later, he returned to the 1956 World Science Fiction Convention (now called WorldCon) to find that attending in costume had become more the norm than not: "Monsters, mutants, scientists, spacemen, aliens and assorted 'Things' thronged the ballroom floor as the flashbulbs popped."

Pretty soon, costumes became an integral part of any science-fiction fan gathering. Some fans dressed in a general fantasy style, like Ackerman; others carefully recreated replica outfits from their favourite films, shows or comics, like Jones.

In order to better fit the growing trend into convention culture, event organizers began arranging a "masquerade". The first masquerade, held at 1940's WorldCon, included dancing and a live band. Costumed attendees were given awards on their craftsmanship at the end of the evening. By 1974, the dancing and music was gone, leaving just the contest. But the name stuck. Today the masquerade remains a costume contest featuring in-character skits, and is still a tradition at anime, comics and science-fiction conventions.

Masquerades continue to be judged according to the divisions set up at WorldCon in 1982: novice, journeyman and master. Entrants choose one of the three divisions, based on their skill level and how long they've

BELOW A FEMALE RENDITION OF THE DEADLY SUB-ZERO FROM VIDEO GAME MORTAL KOMBAT PANTOMIMES HER SIGNATURE ATTACK. PHOTOGRAPHED BY MIKE KOWALEK.

been practising cosplay. Masquerades ensure an emphasis on the art of cosplay, on how well people can emulate a character through both craft and theatrics. Wigs, make-up and props are all considered in the judging process.

Cosplay was steadily growing more popular every year, but there still wasn't a word to describe it. "Futuristicostume" was a mouthful, and as it became more popular for fans to dress up as caped superheroes and anime characters, it was no longer very accurate.

Fast forward to 1984, when Japanese reporter and manga publisher Nobuyuki Takahashi attended Los Angeles WorldCon. He was overwhelmed by fans' arrestingly embellished outfits, as well as the wearers' frequent refusal to break character while in costume. To him, the play-acting element made the hobby a practice to be differentiated from regular old costume wearing. In order to explain it to his Japanese readers, he coined the term "cosplay", a decidedly Japanese contraction of the two English words "costume" and "play".

It's hard to say exactly how cosplay spread to the rest of the world, only that it did – and quickly. Thanks to the Internet, cosplayers found one another in chatrooms and on mailing lists, and the practice took off. Today cosplayers can keep in touch via several different social networks designed just for them: A Cosplay Paradise, World Cosplay, Japan-based Cosplay Cure and others.

Meanwhile, as cosplay grew up privately in Internet chats, the idea of fantasy role-play was continuing to permeate the mainstream psyche. In 1996, on the NBC hit comedy *Friends*, Ross divulged an interest in seeing Rachel dress up in the metal bikini worn by Princess Leia. Needless to say, Leia's *Return of the Jedi* look happened to be one of the most popular cosplays found at any science-fiction convention of that era.

Cosplay finally got its own TV show in 2013, exactly 75 years after Ackerman and Jones changed history at WorldCon. *Heroes of Cosplay* aired on the SyFy channel and documented nine cosplayers as they competed in convention masquerades around the United States. The premiere drew three-quarters of a million viewers, establishing "cosplay" as a household term.

That was just one of the reasons why cosplay, once purely a hobby, has led to lucrative careers for some of its better-known proponents. Arisa Mizuhara, Alodia Gosiengfiao and Yaya Han are three professional cosplayers working out of Japan, the Philippines and the United States respectively. A professional cosplayer may be paid to appear at conventions, sell photo books of her cosplays or sell props she creates. American cosplayer Crystal Graziano has found work on retainer with a video-game company; they come up with outlandish character designs and she makes and models the costumes at their game shows. With all these differing income streams, it's no longer absurd to imagine making a living this way.

However, modern cosplay isn't just about winning contests and making cash. Only a small percentage of cosplay practitioners have professional aspirations. The vast majority of today's cosplayers care most about creating an expression of love for a favourite character. Yaya Han famously told her fans that anything goes in cosplay: "There is no rule book, commandments or memo on *how* you should cosplay. If you want to dress as a character that looks nothing like you, go for it!"

There may be no manual for cosplay, but fans work to a set of etiquette rules on how to treat cosplayers. For example, while it's perfectly all right to run up and hug costumed actors at Disney World, it's not kosher to do the same thing to cosplayers at conventions, even if you recognize them as some of your favourite characters. And no matter how much skin a cosplayer is currently revealing, it's not an invitation to hit on her.

The crux of this message often takes the form of "Cosplay Is Not Consent", a slogan frequently emblazoned on posters at conventions. In the discussion that has followed, cosplayers of both genders have come forward to agree that even though cosplay is about fantasy, it is not about your fantasies. Not only can you damage people's cosplay when you touch them without permission, but you can cross boundaries and hurt feelings too.

This is evidence that members of the cosplay community are learning to treat one another with respect. Another improvement is the general consensus among cosplayers that race, gender, weight and height are all things that don't matter in cosplay. While in earlier times cosplayers were urged to choose characters that were appropriate to their ethnicity or body type, it's been decades since these have been deciding factors in judging cosplay quality.

"I've never understood what would make someone look at an expertly crafted costume and turn their nose up at it because the person wearing it was the 'wrong race'," says

ABOVE *STAVE POISED, SHIYA COSPLAYS SHINO, A CLERIC FROM THE ANIME AND GAME SERIES .HACK. PHOTOGRAPHED BY JOSEPH CHI LIN.*

OPPOSITE *"WHEN I PUT ON A COSTUME I GET A BIT MORE CONFIDENT . . . OF MY IDENTITY AS A PERSON," SAYS JOHNNY "JUNKERS" ZABATE. PHOTOGRAPHED BY JOSEPH CHI LIN.*

ABOVE COSPLAYERS PORTRAYING X-MEN COMIC BOOK HEROES BEAST AND MYSTIQUE TAKE A LEISURELY STROLL AT MCM COMIC CON. PHOTOGRAPHED BY TOLGA AKMEN.

cosplayer Chaka Cumberbatch. "A costume is something you put on. Skin colour is not."

Today cosplay is enjoyed the world over. If a beloved fan character exists, you can bet somebody has made a cosplay of him or her. For every fantasy subculture like gothic, steampunk, cyberpunk or Renaissance Faire, there's at least one cosplayer staying up late at a sewing machine, bringing it to life. Whether the cosplay is a cosplayer's favourite imaginary hero or just a brand-new character that looks cool, anything goes.

"The biggest misconception, to me, is that you have to be an expert at the video game, movie or comic in order to cosplay something," says cosplayer Olivia Chu. "As long as you're genuinely interested in the character, have a good time making and wearing the costume, and are respectful to others, then that is all that matters!"

Modern cosplay isn't the weird curiosity it was once considered to be. Now it's hard to remember cosplay the way it was perceived decades ago, as a niche interest for only the most devoted of science-fiction fans. After noticing that cosplay was regarded with suspicion, and considered even to be evidence of pathology, clinical psychologists Dr Andrea Letamendi and Dr Robin Rosenberg created the "Psychology of Cosplay" survey. Speaking to *Daily Dot* reporter Lisa Granshaw about the survey, Letamendi said: "They cosplay for creativity, to be social and hang out with friends, because they identify with the character and that's meaningful to them. The top reason people cosplay is because it's fun. You can't pinpoint an abnormality in that. It's no different than someone who plays in a band or plays sports."

Speaking of sports, we've all seen superfans at the World Cup slathered in head-to-toe body paint or wearing homemade headdresses as they cheer on their favourite teams. It's not just cosplayers who have discovered that putting on an outfit and acting like somebody else for the day is the ultimate escape. The increasing popularity of cosplay didn't just come out of nowhere; it's simply that now everyone wants to join in the fun.

Cosplay enthusiasts practise their hobby across the globe, elevating the hobby to an art form via make-up and fabric choice, and even through the ways they choose to digitally edit their photos. In this book, we've selected cosplay from all genres and corners of the world to showcase dedicated fans and their fantastic costume design. From pop culture to inspired original looks, the cosplays in this book vary in every way except one – the wearers' undeniable passion for their craft.

FANDOM CONVENTIONS MAKE FOR
PECULIAR COSPLAY ENCOUNTERS.
HERE, COSPLAYERS PORTRAYING
PLAYABLE CHARACTERS FROM THE
MASS EFFECT VIDEO GAME SIT
NEXT TO EMMETT FROM THE LEGO
MOVIE. PHOTOGRAPHED BY TOLGA
AKMEN AT MGM COMIC CON IN
LONDON.

ANIME AND MANGA

KIRO ZISHAN, ZHEN ZHEN MYA, SUTA MISAKI, AND MEGURINE LUKA ENVISION THE MODERN-DAY SWIM TEAM MEMBERS FROM FREE! IN CLASSIC SAILOR UNIFORMS. PHOTOGRAPHED BY MICHAEL OOI.

American fans were cosplaying some 40 years before the hobby found its way to Japan. However, outsiders often mistakenly believe cosplay to be of Japanese origins.

One reason is that, although Japan didn't invent the activity of cosplay, it did invent the term for it. Fan and writer Nobuyuki Takahashi coined the word "cosplay" in his Japanese-language magazine to explain the combination of costuming and play-acting.

Another reason is that Japanese fans adopted "costume play" with equal enthusiasm to their American counterparts around the 1980s. Just as American fans were cosplaying as characters from the TV shows, films and comics they enjoyed most, Japanese geeks began imitating characters from some of their preferred media – anime and manga.

Anime, a Japanese word derived from the English "animation", is a heavily stylized and distinctly Japanese type of animated cartoon. Anime has no one topic or category, but spans many genres, audiences and age groups. Manga is its comic-book compatriot: the same style but in paperback form. Both have global fandoms today, but before the digital age made it easy to stream foreign shows and comics wherever you are, they were most popular in their country of origin.

Early Japanese cosplayers looked to the popular franchises like giant robot-themed *Mobile Suit Gundam* and comic fantasy *Urusai Yatsura* for costume ideas. But cosplay in Japan truly took off in 1984 following the success of *Captain Tsubasa*, a manga-turned-anime series about a soccer team. It was so easy for fans to get their hands on soccer jerseys, why wouldn't they take a chance on the new cosplay fad?

America may have invented cosplay, but Japan soon institutionalized it. An economy quickly built up around materials like wigs and props for helping cosplayers best emulate their desired characters. The first magazine aimed at cosplayers, *Dengeki Layers*, originated in Japan and continues to be published to this day. Since it can be hard to find patterns for the fantastic costumes anime characters wear, this magazine is dedicated to providing custom sewing patterns to help cosplayers match what they see on TV. In 2002, it was joined by *Cosmode*, which is now also available in English. However, the latter is less a how-to than a photo book that showcases talented cosplayers from all over the world.

Perhaps the apex of Japanese cosplay popularity was reached in 1999, when the first cosplay café opened in Akihabara, the nerdiest neighbourhood in Tokyo. The first café is lost to time, but dozens more have popped up, both in Japan and globally, to take its place. Waiting staff are often dressed in embellished maid or butler outfits inspired by anime characters.

Today, cosplayers in Japan have branched out into many other fandoms, including pop idols and video-game protagonists. But anime and manga continue to be their primary choice. At Nagoya Cosplay Summit, costumes inspired by Japanese franchises dominate, even as the event expands globally. When the summit began in 2003, cosplayers from four countries participated. At the 2014 event, competing cosplayers came from more than 20 nations.

Today, you can find anime fans anywhere in the world, and the same goes for anime cosplay. No matter where cosplayers are located, their love of this distinct Japanese art form unites them. Hannah Lees-Kent and Yaya Han live and work on separate coasts of the United States, but their interest in an anime called *Macross Frontier* encouraged them to collaborate and cosplay as two of the main characters, Ranka Lee and Sheryl Nome.

"When Yaya introduced me to the anime, I fell in love with Ranka and really enjoyed her relationship with Sheryl," says Lees-Kent. "So I of course was thrilled when Yaya suggested this cosplay. Yaya and I were able to do our fabric shopping together, which was great for matching textures and patterns for these two looks. We then worked on them separately, on opposite coasts, but sharing our progress along the way. It took me a few months, while working a full-time job, to construct, but I really loved watching it come together."

From stories about high school to high fantasy and futuristic dystopia, anime and manga surpass many different genres, leading to a variety of costuming opportunities for novice and master cosplayers alike. While school uniforms attract beginners with their comparable ease, more advanced seamstresses may opt for ball gowns and evil-heroine getups.

But cosplayers' efforts don't end with the sartorial challenge. Because they are based on cartoon drawings rather than reality, characters often possess gravity-defying hairstyles and unnaturally coloured eyes. Anime and manga are also especially known for their wide-eyed, small-mouthed art style. Cosplayers frequently spend as much time on their wig styling, contact lenses and make-up as on their costume in order to capture that iconic look.

In this chapter, you'll see cosplayers portraying some of anime and manga's most recognizable heroes and heroines. Some of these cosplays are as old as anime itself, dating from even before cosplay hit Japan – like the Speed and Trixie duo from 1960s hit anime *Speed Racer*. Others, like Vampy Bit Me's portrayal of *Mobile Suit Gundam*'s femme fatale Haman, are new renditions of characters people have cosplayed since the '80s.

Others still take their inspiration from modern classics, like *Sailor Moon* or *Neon Genesis Evangelion*. These '90s shows are still considered required reading (or viewing) for novice manga and anime fans, and their characters are staples in fandom lore. Even as hundreds of new anime and manga come out every year, you're bound to see a few of these regulars at any given fandom convention.

Yet others can only be described as cutting-edge. One of the most impressive facets of the cosplay hobby is how cosplayers are able seemingly to churn out elaborate costumes overnight, based on characters in movies that haven't come out yet or TV shows that are still airing. *Attack on Titan* and *Kill La Kill* were two breakout hits from late 2013 and early 2014 that captured cosplayers' imaginations long before they were over, and had already been photographed early and often enough to be featured in this book.

OPPOSITE A FRILLY DRESS AND ALICE BOW, COMBINED WITH AN EDGY VARIEGATED WIG AND GOTHIC STRIPED SOCKS LEND MAYU NYAN THE PERFECT COMBINATION OF INNOCENCE AND SUBVERSION TO PORTRAY STOCKING FROM PANTY & STOCKING WITH GARTERBELT. PHOTOGRAPHED BY THOMAS KUAN.

RIGHT HAYASHI HITOMI IS SITTING PRETTY AS KARUTA, A SWEET-TOOTHED TEEN FROM INU X BOKU SS, THE SUPERNATURAL COMEDY ROMANCE. PHOTOGRAPHED BY THOMAS KUAN

ABOVE YINC TAN IS CUTE AND DANGEROUS AS TOKISAKI KURUMI, A GIRL WITH MYSTERIOUS POWERS FROM DATE A LIVE. TRICK PHOTOGRAPHY MAKES TAN APPEAR AS WEIGHTLESS AS THE SPIRIT CHARACTER SHE IS COSPLAYING. PHOTOGRAPHED BY MICHAEL OOI.

OPPOSITE KAZUMI NAO GETS INTO CHARACTER AS YAZAWA NICO, THE BUBBLY HIGH SCHOOL IDOL SINGER FROM LOVE LIVE! SCHOOL IDOL PROJECT. PHOTOGRAPHED BY MICHAEL OOI.

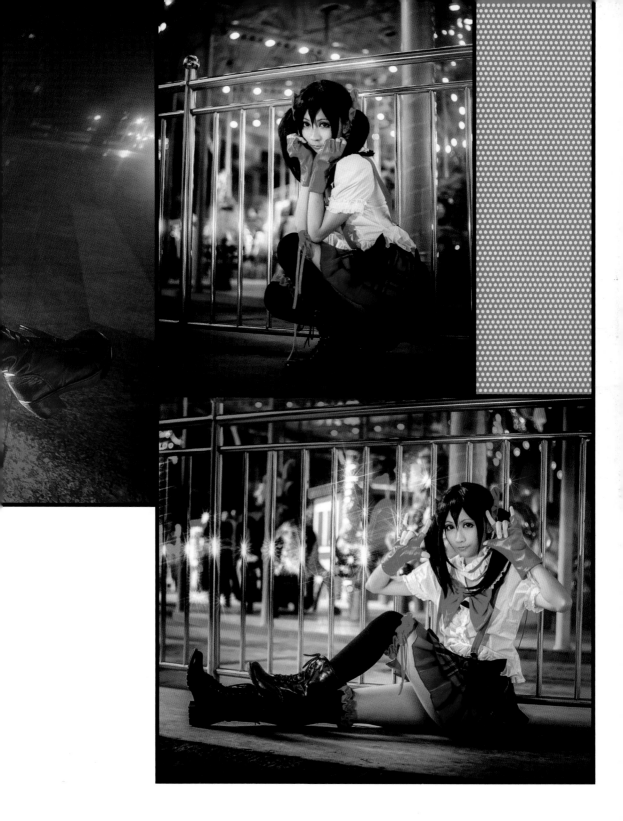

LEFT AND BELOW KYU-ERIEN IS DRESSED AS YUI, THE PINK-HAIRED LEAD SINGER OF THE AFTERLIFE FROM ANGEL BEATS! PHOTOGRAPHED BY MICHAEL OOI.

OPPOSITE YUTAKA MIDORI WEARS ONE BLUE CONTACT AND ONE GREEN CONTACT TO ACCURATELY MIMIC NEKO, THE MISCHIEVOUS CATGIRL FROM K PROJECT. PHOTOGRAPHED BY THOMAS KUAN.

BELOW IN SUMPTUOUS VELVET, YAYA HAN IS CARMILLA, THE ARISTOCRATIC VAMPIRE QUEEN OF *VAMPIRE HUNTER D. SHE DESCRIBED THE CONSTRUCTION PROCESS ON HER BLOG: "I WAS VERY PICKY WITH MY FABRICS BECAUSE THE CHARACTER IS SO ELEGANTLY DECADENT, I WANTED THE COSTUME TO LOOK RICH AND LUXURIOUS. I WENT WITH 25 OR SO YARDS* OF DEEP RED MADONNA VELVET, WHICH FRUSTRATINGLY IS A HARD FABRIC TO WORK WITH BECAUSE IT FRAYS SO MUCH AND LIKES TO MOVE AROUND WHILE YOU SEW IT." THIS COSTUME WON THE GRAND PRIZE AT NEW YORK ANIME FEST 2009, EARNING HAN A TRIP TO JAPAN. PHOTOGRAPHED BY JUDITH STEPHENS AT ANIME USA 2009.

LEFT HANNAH LEES-KENT
AS RANKA LEE AND YAYA
HAN AS SHERYL NOME
DON TECHNICOLOUR
KIMONOS TO CAPTURE
THE FUTURISTIC FANTASY
OF MACROSS FRONTIER.
"IT WAS MY FIRST TIME
WORKING WITH HORSEHAIR,
BUT I ADORE THE HUGE
RUFFLES IT ADDED TO THE
SKIRT," LEES-KENT SAID.
"I ALSO HAD NEVER WORN
CONTACTS BEFORE, BUT
FELT IT WAS IMPORTANT TO
WEAR RED ONES FOR THIS
CHARACTER, AS IT HUGELY
CONTRASTED SHERYL'S
BLUE EYES." PHOTOGRAPHED
AT ANIME EXPO BY MARTIN
WONG.

OPPOSITE LINDA LE, ALSO
KNOWN AS VAMPY BIT ME
IN THE COSPLAY WORLD,
COMMANDS THE ZEON
FLEET AS HAMAN, THE
TRAGIC VILLAINESS FROM
MOBILE SUIT ZETA GUNDAM.
PHOTOGRAPHED BY LONG
THAI AT ANIME MATSURI
2014 IN HOUSTON, TEXAS.

ABOVE DIA (LEFT) AND CHRISTOPHER P. NGUYEN ARE READY TO RACE AS TRIXIE AND SPEED RACER, TWO CLASSIC ANIME CHARACTERS FROM THE '60s HIT SPEED RACER. PHOTOGRAPHED AT KATSUCON 2011 BY NICOLE CIARAMELLA.

OPPOSITE BOWSTRING TAUT, SERENE TEO AIMS HER BEAUTY SERENE ARROW AS CHACHA, THE TITULAR HEROINE FROM CLASSIC SHOUJO ANIME AKAZUKIN CHACHA. PHOTOGRAPHED BY THOMAS KUAN.

LEFT A PLAYFUL ATTITUDE AND LOTS OF RED VINYL ARE THE KEYS TO ASTAROHIME KOYU'S COSPLAY AS THE TITULAR CHARACTER SAKURA FROM CARDCAPTOR SAKURA. PHOTOGRAPHED IN MOSCOW BY ALENA PUGOFFKA.

OPPOSITE AND ABOVE IN A PLUGSUIT
TAILORED TO HER EVERY CURVE, FROSEL
IS ASUKA LANGLEY SORYU, THE GERMAN-
JAPANESE MECHA PILOT FROM NEON GENESIS
EVANGELION. PHOTOGRAPHED IN MOSCOW BY
ALENA PUGOFFKA.

LEFT MERVYN "THE BACONATOR" LIM TAKES A BREAK FROM HIS OWN COSPLAY PHOTOGRAPHY TO BE PHOTOGRAPHED BY THOMAS KUAN. LIM IS DRESSED AS THE GREAT KING EMMA FROM DARK COMEDY SERIES HOZUKI NO REITETSU.

OPPOSITE LOUD YELLOW VINYL HELPS KATIE COSPLAYS STAND OUT IN A CROWD AS FAYE VALENTINE, THE INCORRIGIBLE CON-WOMAN FROM COWBOY BEBOP. PHOTOGRAPHED BY JOSEPH CHILLIN.

RIGHT MRDUSTINN AND
PRISCILLA COSPLAY ARE
MIRROR IMAGES OF EACH
OTHER AS A MALE AND
FEMALE VERSION OF
THE SAME CHARACTER,
MAKO FROM KILL LA
KILL. COSPLAY GIVES
FANS THE FREEDOM TO
INTERPRET CHARACTERS
IN VARYING WAYS,
INCLUDING ENVISIONING
THE CHARACTER WITH
A DIFFERENT GENDER.
PHOTOGRAPHED BY
ERIC NG.

OPPOSITE DYNAMICALLY POSED, DERPCARO IS NO REGULAR SCHOOLGIRL AS RYUKO MATOI FROM KILL LA KILL. PHOTOGRAPHED AT ANIME NORTH IN TORONTO, CANADA BY MIKE KOWALEK.

ABOVE THE CLOTHES MAKE THE MAN IN YUTAMORI'S COSPLAY AS UZU SANAGEYAMA FROM KILL LA KILL, AN ANIME ALL ABOUT THE POWER OF CLOTHING. PHOTOGRAPHED IN KIEV, UKRAINE BY ALENA PUGOFFKA.

LEFT NICOLE CIARAMELLA PHOTOGRAPHED AN ENTIRE SOLAR SYSTEM OF SAILOR SCOUTS IN A WOODLAND CLEARING IN AFTON, NEW YORK. FROM LEFT TO RIGHT: CARLY, CHRIS [TRIANGLES], MELLY, YUFFIEBUNNY, UMISTER, AMBROSIA KRYS, CLAIRE [COSMICANDLOVE], MOIRA [ARKWRIGHT] AND STARDUSTSHADOW.

BELOW JAYUNA (LEFT), GILLYKINS, OLIVIASATELIER, HONEYSALIVA AND REDRIBBONCOSPLAY DO THEIR OWN TAKE ON THE GIRL-POWERED SAILOR SCOUTS OF SAILOR MOON. PHOTOGRAPHED AT ANIME NORTH IN TORONTO, CANADA BY MIKE KOWALEK.

COSPLAYER JINRI PARK'S
TAILORED DRESS AND
FLOWING WIG, COMBINED
WITH PHOTOGRAPHER JASON
TABLANTE'S POST-PRODUCTION
EFFECTS, MAKE FOR AN
OTHERWORLDLY SAILOR MARS
FROM SAILOR MOON.

OPPOSITE TINA LAM, WHO ALSO GOES BY TURN ON RED, PORTRAYS THE BIZARRE BUT DEADLY OKTAVIA VON SECKENDORFF FROM MADOKA MAGICA. PHOTOGRAPHED AT KATSUCON BY ANNA FISCHER.

BELOW KUBRA KAZANCI AND ZEYNEP TANIKOGLU POSE AS ETERNAL FRIENDS HOMURA AND MADOKA FROM THE GENRE-FLIPPING MAGICAL GIRL ANIME MADOKA MAGICA. PHOTOGRAPHED AT TORUCON BY ALTUG ISLER.

OPPOSITE AND RIGHT
HUGE HAIRBOWS
AND A FLUFFY PINK
PETTICOAT TO
MATCH HER WIG
MAKE CHRISTY KIM
A CHARMING AND
CHEERFUL MIWAKO,
THE FASHION MAVEN
OF THE PARADISE
KISS SERIES.
PHOTOGRAPHED IN
ATLANTA, GEORGIA BY
BENNY LEE.

ABOVE AND OPPOSITE WOVEN WITH BLUE ROSES, VINAKULA'S WIG DRAPES OVER HER BEADED BALLGOWN TO REACH THE FLOOR. SHE AND FELLOW COSPLAYER DAISUKE PORTRAY YUKARI AND GEORGE, THE STAR-CROSSED FASHION MODELS AT THE CENTRE OF *PARADISE KISS.* PHOTOGRAPHED IN MOSCOW BY ALENA PUGOFFKA.

ABOVE TOMMEHCHU IS BURSTING WITH ENTHUSIASM AS HAZAMA MASAYOSHI, THE MALE MODEL AND ASPIRING SUPERHERO FROM SAMURAI FLAMENCO. PHOTOGRAPHED AT ANIME NORTH IN TORONTO, CANADA BY MIKE KOWALEK.

RIGHT WITH HER KATANA AT HER SIDE, DAMIENA COSPLAYS AS KUCHIKI BYAKUYA, A BENEVOLENT GOD OF DEATH FROM THE EXPLOSIVELY POPULAR ANIME BLEACH. BYAKUYA IS KNOWN AS AN ESPECIALLY BEAUTIFUL MALE CHARACTER, WHICH MAKES HIM AN IDEAL SUBJECT FOR A FEMALE "CROSSPLAYERS". PHOTOGRAPHED IN MOSCOW BY ALENA PUGOFFKA.

BELOW ACCOMPANIED BY PLUSH MONSTER COMPANIONS, ERIN [FIREWOLF826] (LEFT) AND AMANDA [BLUUCIRCLES] DRESS AS KEN AND DAVIS FROM DIGIMON ADVENTURE 02. PHOTOGRAPHED IN BRYANT PARK, NEW YORK CITY BY NICOLE CIARAMELLA.

RIGHT LUFFY THE PIRATE MAY BE MALE IN HIS ANIME, ONE PIECE, BUT COSPLAY ALLOWS FANS TO TAKE CREATIVE LICENCE WITH THAT SORT OF THING. JENNI [MOSTFLOGGED] WAVES THE PIRATE FLAG ON CONEY ISLAND, NEW YORK. "I WORE GENDERBEND LUFFY AT A PRIVATE SHOOT, THAT COSTUME HAS NEVER HIT A CONVENTION FLOOR! HOWEVER, A FEW PEOPLE DID RECOGNIZE ME AT THE BEACH WE SHOT AT," SHE SAID. PHOTOGRAPHED BY NICOLE CIARAMELLA.

OPPOSITE DARDENSEBOY (LEFT) AND KINIRO-ONIBA ARE DRESSED AS REPTILE-TYPE MONSTER GUILMON AND BEAST-TYPE MONSTER LEOMON FROM DIGIMON, A SHOW WHERE KIDS TRAIN AND COLLABORATE WITH DIGITAL MONSTERS. PHOTOGRAPHED AT ANIME NORTH IN TORONTO, CANADA BY MIKE KOWALEK.

BELOW MR. FROGGLE (LEFT), PSYCHOSCARF, AND TRINATION ARE ORIGAMI CYCLONE, DRAGON KID, AND BLUE ROSE – SUPERHEROES FROM THE WORLD OF TIGER & BUNNY. PHOTOGRAPHED AT OTAKUTHON IN MONTREAL, CANADA BY MIKE KOWALEK.

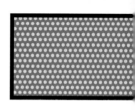

BELOW SHER MYN, KUMI HANAKO, VIVIEN YEE, YUI MIKI AND ELYON LIM ARE READY TO ROCK AS THE HIGH SCHOOL GIRL BAND FROM THE SHOW K-ON!. PHOTOGRAPHED BY MICHAEL OOI.

OPPOSITE MERU (LEFT), KATIE AND SAMANTHA JOKE AROUND AS TAIGA, MINORI AND AMI, THE THREE MAIN HEROINES FROM THE COMEDY ROMANCE TORADORA. PHOTOGRAPHED IN ATLANTA, GEORGIA BY BENNY LEE.

ABOVE THIS LONDON FILM AND COMIC CON ATTENDEE HAS SEAMLESSLY MERGED HER FACEPAINT AND BODYSUIT IN ORDER TO PORTRAY COMBAT-READY ANNIE, A TITAN-SHIFTER AND MAIN VILLAINESS FROM ATTACK ON TITAN. PHOTOGRAPHED BY GUY BELL.

LEFT HAKUKU AND AKUSESU ARE LOVE INTERESTS AND HUMANITY'S ONLY HOPES WHILE THEY BATTLE TITANS AS EREN AND MIKASA FROM ATTACK ON TITAN. SPECIAL EFFECTS CREATED BY ERIC NG.

RIGHT JOHNNY "JUNKERS" ZABATE
LETS OUT A ROAR AS GUTS, THE
HEAVILY ARMOURED PROTAGONIST
OF BERSERK. "FULL BODY ARMORS
USUALLY TAKE THREE FULL WEEKS
OF WORK," HE SAYS. "PEOPLE
USUALLY THINK THAT AS A COUPLE
OF HOURS AFTER WORK, BUT WHEN
I SAY THREE FULL WEEKS I MEAN
THREE WEEKS OF TWELVE-HOUR DAYS
AND NO WEEKENDS. IT'S DIFFICULT
STUFF." PHOTOGRAPHED BY ERIC NG.

ABOVE AN ELABORATE HEADDRESS AND ELEGANT
GOWN MAKE LAUZ LANILLE LOOK EVERY INCH THE
IMPERIAL PRINCESS KOUGYOKU REN FROM MAGI:
THE LABYRINTH OF MAGIC. PHOTOGRAPHED BY ALENA
PUGOFFKA AT SALON DEL MANGA, AN ANIME FANDOM
CONVENTION IN BARCELONA, SPAIN.

LEFT THERE'S NO MORE ACCURATE SETTING FOR KIRO
ZISHAN, ZHEN ZHEN MYA, SUTA MISAKI AND MEGURINE
LUKA TO SHOW OFF THEIR SAILOR COSPLAY AS
THE SWIM TEAM FROM FREE! THAN THE SEASIDE.
PHOTOGRAPHED BY MICHAEL OOI.

LEFT NG CHEOK NEY IS RYUKO MATOI, THE SCHOOL GIRL WITH AN ATTITUDE AND A MISSION FROM 2014'S BREAKOUT HIT KILL LA KILL. PHOTOGRAPHED BY MICHAEL OOI.

RIGHT POSING WITH A RIFLE TALLER THAN SHE IS, AN ANIME CENTRAL 2011 COSPLAYER PERSONIFIES THE CAPABLE, CHEERFUL MARKSWOMAN FROM GURREN LAGANN. PHOTOGRAPHED BY JUDITH STEPHENS.

BELOW AMETHYSTPRINCE (LEFT), ICHI, AND INDIGOHOLLOW COSPLAY AS SWIMMERS HARUKA NANASE, RIN MATSUOKA, AND MAKOTO TACHIBANA FROM THE SWIMMING ANIME FREE!. HERE, BODY LANGUAGE AND BODY CONTOURING MAKEUP ARE A KEY PART OF PORTRAYING THE CHARACTERS. PHOTOGRAPHED IN MOSCOW BY ALENA PUGOFFKA.

LEFT GUN COCKED, MAKI ROLL IS READY FOR ACTION AS KEI, A COP WITH A REPUTATION FOR COLLATERAL DAMAGE, FROM THE CLASSIC ANIME DIRTY PAIR. PHOTOGRAPHED BY ANNA FISCHER.

RIGHT MEEPY-GAL POSES AS REI AYANAMI IN A SKINTIGHT PLUGSUIT – THE FLIGHT SUIT UNIQUE TO THE WORLD OF NEON GENESIS EVANGELION. MEEPY IS SO WELL KNOWN FOR HER PLUGSUIT CRAFTSMANSHIP THAT SHE HAS PUBLISHED A BOOK FOR COSPLAYERS ON CONSTRUCTING SIMILAR COSTUMES. PHOTOGRAPHED AT SAKURACON BY ERIC NG.

SCIENCE FICTION FANTASIES

GOLD-PLATED ARMOUR AND A DRAMATIC
HELM ADORN KAMUI AS SHE CHANNELS
X-MEN'S DANI MOONSTAR, A MUTANT
WITH THE ABILITY TO CREATE ILLUSIONS.
PHOTOGRAPHED BY NICOLE CIARAMELLA AT
NEW YORK COMIC CON 2014.

Heroes and villains. *The Avengers* and *X-Men*. *Star Wars* and *Star Trek*. Cosplay that takes its cues from science fiction is some of the hobby's most recognizable, but also some of the most out-of-this-world. If cosplay as a whole is about escaping yourself, science-fiction cosplay is also about escaping the bounds of the universe.

It's no coincidence that the first TV show about cosplay aired on the SyFy channel. *Heroes of Cosplay* fitted right in between shows like *Stargate Atlantis* and *Battlestar Galactica*. After all, who's to say that the fantasy world of cosplay is any less surreal than an interstellar drama? Audiences didn't disagree, and the show was a hit.

When you're not browsing cable, your best bet for catching a glimpse of science-fiction styles is at fandom conventions. The earliest fandom conventions centred around science fiction and comic books, since these are some of the oldest and most accessible fandoms. What's truly astounding is how these costumes have remained popular today.

At comic conventions around the world, you'll still see a hefty showing of what was cosplay's original look – heroes and heroines from the future. Following in the footsteps of Forrest J. Ackerman and Myrtle R. Jones, the pair of science-fiction fans who are credited as the world's first cosplayers after gracing 1939's World Science Fiction Convention with their galactic garb, cosplayers have never stopped imagining their own visions of the twenty-third century.

More than 70 years after superheroes first graced the covers of comic books, they're still a science-fiction-convention staple. You're always sure to see heroes like Superman, Batman and Spiderman; villians like Deadpool, Madame Hydra and the Joker; and more classics from Marvel and DC comics alike. Especially after the popularity of the *Avengers* franchise, you'll be bound to see metal-suited Iron Men, scarlet-haired Black Widows and slyly sneering Lokis. However, cosplayers don't shy away from more obscure heroes – either as a testament to their fantastic character designs or as a calling card to other comic buffs in an indication of the cosplayer's knowledge and interests.

Star Wars is another establishment of geek culture that has had a long-running legacy in cosplay. From Chewbacca's furry face to Leia's metal bikini, outfits and props of the decades-old movies are instantly recognizable and lead to costumes that guarantee a reaction. One of the most famous group of *Star Wars* cosplayers is the 501st Legion, a global organization of *Star Wars* fans who dress up as stormtroopers, often while doing good. You might see the 501st show up in style at a fandom convention to host a blood drive, raise money for charity, or simply entertain visitors with their matching uniforms.

Likewise, *Star Trek* is an easily identified convention cosplay staple. Decades after Captain Kirk first vowed to boldly go where no man had gone before, you can still meet people dressed like him. Uniforms from the original series, *Star Trek: The Next Generation* and spin-off series like *Deep Space Nine* are easy to purchase prefab, so they make a simple, easily constructed costume for cosplay beginners. On the other hand, the clean lines of *Star Trek*'s futuristic apparel make a good base for experienced cosplayers looking to tailor clothes to their exact specifications. Experienced or not, a cosplayer in uniform is unlikely to be the only one at the convention. And, as with *Star Wars* and superhero teams, it can be gratifying to show up at a con and find that you're already part of a team.

As technology marches on, it's not just cosplay ideas that come from the future. Construction techniques for building cosplay costume parts have become equally high-tech. Natasha Spokish, who goes by the name of Bindi Smalls in the cosplay world, creates props using 3D printing, a process for making physical objects out of 3D computer models she designs herself.

"Once I received my first 3D printed item, I knew I was hooked," says Spokish. "The quality was impeccable, and I felt as if I had learned a valuable skill. We purchased our first printer shortly thereafter and haven't looked back since."

Today, Spokish runs a booming 3D printing business, designing and printing gauntlets, helms and swords for cosplayers portraying characters from any time period, not just the future.

"3D printing is catching on faster than I expected, because the cosplay community is very diverse and cosplayers tend to have many skills," she says. "There are quite a few cosplayers who are already making 3D models and have embraced 3D printing, as well as engineers and engineering students who may already have access to a 3D printer at work or school. There are definitely still a fair amount of sceptics in the community – or people who wholeheartedly prefer handmade items. But once they see the possibilities and understand the work involved in 3D printing for cosplay, they tend to change their minds."

Another high-tech cosplay innovation you'll see in this book is post-production special effects. Jason Tablante uses Photoshop – a computer program for enhancing photos – to create photo backdrops which are just as fantastic as the cosplayers' hand-crafted outfits that he photographs. Glowing rays of lights and aerial backdrops can transform an earthbound cosplayer into a soaring superhero.

Today, Tablante uses Photoshop as the finishing touch on his photos to make them look even more incredible. But it's hardly the only technique he employs to achieve the final shot, and he says he discourages cosplay photographers from using it as a shortcut instead of learning the basics.

"The immediate and probably the obvious conclusion for most people for hyper-realistic images is the usage of Photoshop. But I would beg to disagree that it's the only way to achieve these effects," he says. "Photoshop is nothing but the final touch during the last mile of creating these images. A good portion of our work still relies on good old camera tricks and practical effects."

In this chapter, you'll see men and women dressed as some of the science-fiction pantheon's most iconic superheroes, supervillians, adventurers and sentient robots. Hopefully you'll also discover new characters you've never seen before, and be swayed into unearthing their stories after being enchanted by their illustrious appearances. After all, that's what drew so many cosplayers into creating these costumes in the first place.

ABOVE *LED LIGHTS GIVE AN OTHERWORLDLY GLOW TO THE EYES OF THESE JAWA FROM STAR WARS. SHORT OF STATURE IN EASY-TO-EMULATE HOODED ROBES, THE JAWA RACE MAKE A GREAT COSPLAY FOR KIDS. PHOTOGRAPHED BY ALBERT L ORTEGA.*

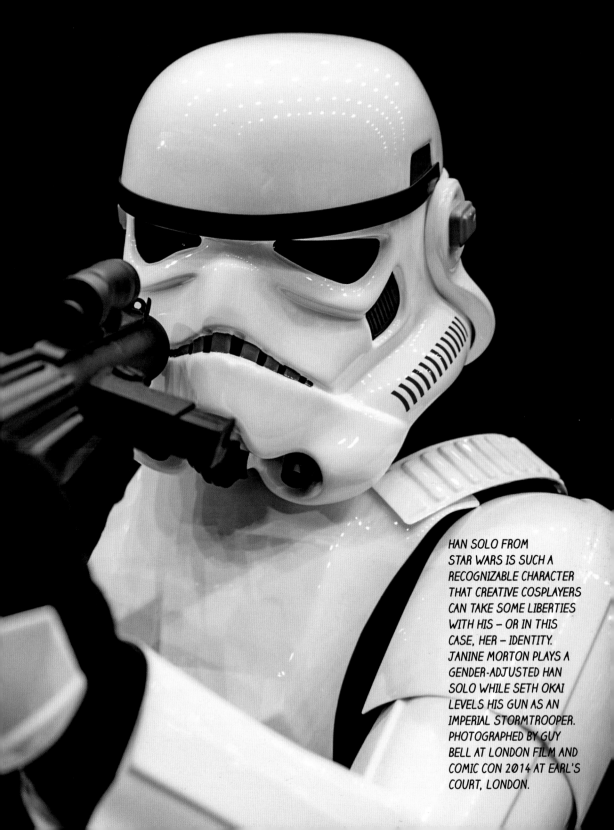

HAN SOLO FROM
STAR WARS IS SUCH A
RECOGNIZABLE CHARACTER
THAT CREATIVE COSPLAYERS
CAN TAKE SOME LIBERTIES
WITH HIS – OR IN THIS
CASE, HER – IDENTITY.
JANINE MORTON PLAYS A
GENDER-ADJUSTED HAN
SOLO WHILE SETH OKAI
LEVELS HIS GUN AS AN
IMPERIAL STORMTROOPER.
PHOTOGRAPHED BY GUY
BELL AT LONDON FILM AND
COMIC CON 2014 AT EARL'S
COURT, LONDON.

LEFT, BELOW AND OPPOSITE ORDINARILY YOU WOULD NEVER SEE MORTAL ENEMIES LIKE STAR WARS' HAN SOLO, AN IMPERIAL STORMTROOPER, AND DARTH MAUL IN ONE PLACE, BUT ANYTHING GOES AT LONDON FILM AND COMIC CON. PHOTOGRAPHED BY GUY BELL.

OPPOSITE AND RIGHT RESISTANCE IS
FUTILE! SYNTHETIC PROSTHETICS AND A
SOULLESS GAZE METAMORPHOSE MILD-
MANNERED COSPLAYER THOR PENDRAGON
INTO A MEMBER OF THE BORG, STAR TREK'S
INFAMOUS ANTAGONISTIC CYBERNETIC RACE.
PHOTOGRAPHED BY GUY BELL AT LONDON
FILM AND COMIC CON 2014.

LEFT WHEN IT COMES TO COSPLAYING THE GOD OF THUNDER, A FEARLESS ATTITUDE IS JUST AS IMPORTANT AS A DYNAMIC COSTUME. COSPLAYER MARK SMITH GETS IN CHARACTER AS THOR DURING THE 2014 NEW YORK COMIC CON. PHOTO BY NEILSON BARNARD.

BELOW THE GANG'S ALL HERE WITH THIS
GROUP COSPLAY OF MORE THAN 20 OF
MARVEL'S MOST ICONIC SUPERHEROES.
EVEN STAN LEE (CENTRE) WANTED TO JOIN
IN ON THIS GATHERING. PHOTOGRAPHED AT
DRAGONCON 2011 BY JUDITH STEPHENS.

ABOVE AND OPPOSITE ANY COMIC BOOK FAN
WOULD RECOGNIZE CAPTAIN AMERICA, NO
MATTER WHETHER COSPLAYERS CHOOSE
TO PORTRAY THIS PATRIOTIC SUPERHERO IN
MALE OR FEMALE FORM. FEMALE CAPTAIN
AMERICA PHOTOGRAPHED BY GUY BELL
AT LONDON FILM AND COMIC CON 2014;
COMIC CON ATTENDEE DAN SCANLON
PHOTOGRAPHED AT NEW YORK COMIC CON
2014 BY NEILSON BARNARD.

LEFT JENNI [MOSTFLOGGED] FLEXES
HER MUSCLES AS THE SUPERPOWERED
MS. MARVEL AT NEW YORK COMIC CON.
PHOTOGRAPHED BY NICOLE CIARAMELLA.

ABOVE VINTAGE TAILORING AND REAL
FEATHER WINGS ADD A GOLDEN AGE FEEL
TO MAGGIE KLIMENTOVA HAWKGIRL
COSTUME. PHOTOGRAPHED AT NEW YORK
COMIC CON 2014 BY NEILSON BARNARD.

OPPOSITE COSPLAYERS HAVE
TAKEN INSPIRATION FROM
SPIDERMAN'S COSTUMES SINCE
THE '60s. THIS COSTUME BY
SHAWN WEBBER IS INSPIRED
BY SPIDERMAN'S MOST RECENT
BIG SCREEN APPEARANCE.
PHOTOGRAPHED AT NEW YORK
COMIC CON 2014 BY NEILSON
BARNARD.

OPPOSITE *LASSO AT THE READY, HELENE WALDERMARSON IS READY TO FIGHT CRIME AS WONDER WOMAN. PHOTOGRAPHED AT NEW YORK COMIC CON BY NEILSON BARNARD.*

ABOVE *JASON WILKINSON OF TITAN COSPLAY USES BODY CONTOURING TO GREAT EFFECT AS PLANET HULK. PHOTOGRAPHED BY LONG THAI AT COMICPALOOZA 2014 IN HOUSTON, TEXAS.*

OPPOSITE FOUR COSPLAYERS MODEL THEIR
BURLESQUE RENDITIONS OF "DC COMICS
BOMBSHELLS" – TWINKLEBAT (LEFT) AS
MERA, YAYA HAN AS ZATANNA, YASHUNTAFUN
COSPLAY AS SUPERGIRL, AND JESSIE L.
AS BLACK CANARY. PHOTOGRAPHED AT
DRAGONCON 2014 BY JUDITH STEPHENS.

ABOVE YASHUNTAFUN AS SUPERGIRL BY
JUDITH STEPHENS.

OPPOSITE *PHOTOGRAPHER JASON TABLANTE USED POST PRODUCTION SPECIAL EFFECTS TO TRANSFORM COSPLAYER ALODIA GOSIENGFIAO INTO X-MEN HEROINE WHITE PHOENIX. PHOTOGRAPHED IN MANILA, PHILIPPINES.*

ABOVE *MIRACOLE BURNS IS WONDER WOMAN, DEFENDER OF THEMYSCIRA, IN ELABORATE FOAM ACCESSORIES PAINTED TO LOOK LIKE METAL. PHOTOGRAPHED BY ANNA FISCHER.*

BELOW COSPLAY PHOTOGRAPHER LONG THAI ENCOUNTERED THE '90s ERA X-MEN AT DALLAS COMIC-CON 2014. FROM LEFT TO RIGHT: SHOE COSPLAY AS MYSTIQUE, TRACIE ADAMS OF KIKALA COSPLAY AS SHADOWCAT, JAMES HARVILL AS CYCLOPS, AND TWINS HOPE AND HEATHER SMITH OF TWINZIK COSPLAY AS ROGUE AND TOAD.

OPPOSITE TOP NOTCH TAILORING AND SPECIAL EFFECTS TRANSFORM RHIAN RAMOS HOWELL INTO X-MEN'S ROGUE IN FLIGHT. PHOTOGRAPHED BY JASON TABLANTE IN MANILA, PHILIPPINES.

ABOVE BLUE FACEPAINT AND POINTED EAR PROSTHETICS LEND A MUTANT FEEL TO THIS NIGHTCRAWLER COSTUME. PHOTOGRAPHED BY GUY BELL AT LONDON FILM AND COMIC CON 2014.

LEFT WITH A BROAD WINGSPAN AND TRADEMARK BLACK AND YELLOW SUIT, MATTHEW WEBB IS ANGEL FROM X-MEN. PHOTOGRAPHED BY GUY BELL AT LONDON FILM AND COMIC CON 2014.

OPPOSITE YOU DON'T HAVE TO BE A CLAIRVOYANT TO TELL THAT IT TOOK HOURS OF CONSTRUCTION TIME TO CREATE KEARSIN FAY NICHOLSON'S COSPLAY AS X-MEN'S PSYCHIC SUPERHERO JEAN GREY. PHOTOGRAPHED BY JOSEPH CHI LIN.

ABOVE COSPLAY RUNS IN THE FAMILY
FOR ANDY AND HIS SON TRYSTAN.
HERE, THEY BOTH WIELD THEIR
ADAMANTIUM CLAWS AS WOLVERINE.
PHOTOGRAPHED BY GUY BELL.

OPPOSITE WITH VINYL ACCESSORIES AND
A DYNAMIC POSE, JENNI [MOSTFLOGGED]
IS THE X-MEN SERIES' FEARLESS
PSIONIC NINJA PSYLOCKE. "COSPLAYING
IS A WAY FOR ME TO EXPRESS MY
LOVE FOR A CHARACTER, A SERIES, A
THEME, A DESIGN, AND SOMETIMES IT'S
JUST TO HAVE FUN WITH FRIENDS! A
LOT OF PEOPLE WHO DON'T COSPLAY
DON'T UNDERSTAND THAT THERE ISN'T
ONE SPECIFIC REASON THAT PEOPLE
COSPLAY, IT'S A MEDLEY OF REASONS
AND IT'S OFTEN DIFFERENT FOR EACH
COSTUME FOR EACH PERSON," SHE SAYS.
PHOTOGRAPHED BY NICOLE CIARAMELLA AT
NEW YORK COMIC CON 2014.

OPPOSITE AND ABOVE GOLD-PLATED ARMOUR AND A DRAMATIC HELM ADORN KAMUI AS SHE CHANNELS X-MEN'S DANI MOONSTAR, A MUTANT WITH THE ABILITY TO CREATE ILLUSIONS. PHOTOGRAPHED BY NICOLE CIARAMELLA AT NEW YORK COMIC CON 2014.

BELOW COSPLAY GAVE THESE TEENAGE MUTANT NINJA TURTLE FANS A CHANCE TO ENVISION THEIR FAVOURITE HEROES IN THE HALF SHELL AS IF THEY WERE THEIR OWN GENDER. FROM LEFT TO RIGHT: JOANNA BERRY AS RAPHAEL, QUAZZIE DAYRIT AS LEONARDO, AIMEE AMPAYA OF FOA COSPLAY AS DONATELLO, AND EMILY MARTENS OF KAIDA CREATIONS AS MICHELANGELO. PHOTOGRAPHED AT COMICPALOOZA 2014 BY LONG THAI.

IN LEATHER, CHAINMAIL AND FUR,
ASHLEY RIOT IS IN HER ELEMENT
AS RED SONJA, THE HIGH FANTASY
HEROINE FROM THE EPONYMOUS
COMIC BOOKS. PHOTOGRAPHED IN
SAN DIEGO BY JASON TABLANTE.

OPPOSITE JIMMY BURNS WEARS A MASK WITH GLOWING EYE HOLES TO PERSONIFY BRIAREOS HECATONCHIRES, THE CYBORG HERO OF APPLESEED. PHOTOGRAPHED BY MARTIN WONG.

BELOW COSPLAYER LIONEL LUM AND FRIEND DON ENORMOUS ARMOURED SUITS TO CONVEY BUMBLEBEE AND IRONHIDE, TWO OF THE SENTIENT ROBOTS FROM TRANSFORMERS. PHOTOGRAPHED AT FANIMECON BY JUDITH STEPHENS.

LEFT IN RED CURLS AND AN IVY EMBELLISHED CORSET, OLIVIA CHU IS A PINUP POISON IVY. "COSPLAY IS ALL ABOUT CONTINUALLY IMPROVING YOUR SKILLS AND LEARNING NEW THINGS WHILE USING YOUR CREATIVITY," SHE SAYS. PHOTOGRAPHED IN NEW JERSEY BY ANNA FISCHER.

OPPOSITE GILLYKINS WEARS HER LEAFY GREENS AS POISON IVY FROM BATMAN: THE ANIMATED SERIES. "I WAS OBSESSED WITH POISON IVY WHEN I WAS LITTLE, I WOULD WANT TO WATCHED THE EPISODES WITH HER OVER AND OVER AGAIN," SHE SAYS. PHOTOGRAPHED AT NEW YORK COMIC CON BY MIKE KOWALEK.

OPPOSITE IN RED AND BLACK FAUX LEATHER, AMMIECHAN IS LOOKING FOR TROUBLE AS PERKY, PSYCHOTIC BATMAN VILLAIN HARLEY QUINN. PHOTOGRAPHED AT ANIME NORTH IN TORONTO, CANADA BY MIKE KOWALEK.

LEFT IN A LOUD PAISLEY SUIT, MARK GASCOINGNE PLAYS AN ESPECIALLY WILD VERSION OF BATMAN'S QUIRKIEST RIVAL, THE JOKER. PHOTOGRAPHED BY GUY BELL AT LONDON FILM AND COMIC CON 2014.

OPPOSITE AND BELOW GIN IS
A DEAD RINGER FOR LOKI, THE
TROUBLEMAKER TRICKSTER
GOD OF THE MARVEL UNIVERSE.
PHOTOGRAPHED BY ALENA PUGOFFKA
IN MOSCOW.

OPPOSITE BEDECKED IN
A BAROQUE-ERA GOWN
AND MASK, A COSPLAYER
PORTRAYS ONE OF THE
MONSTROUS VERSAILLES
INHABITANTS FROM A
FAMOUS DOCTOR WHO
EPISODE, "THE GIRL
IN THE FIREPLACE".
PHOTOGRAPHED AT THE
SCI-FI LONDON FESTIVAL
COSTUME PARADE BY
MATTHEW CHATTLE.

RIGHT A COSPLAYER
TRANSFORMS INTO
A MACHINERY-DRIVEN
CYBERMAN FROM DOCTOR
WHO AT CHICAGO COMIC
AND ENTERTAINMENT
EXPO. PHOTOGRAPHED BY
DANIEL BOCZARSKI.

LEFT AND OPPOSITE
THIS COSPLAYER'S
DRESS IS BIGGER ON
THE INSIDE – IT'S
A GOWN PAINTED
TO RESEMBLE
THE TARDIS, THE
TIME MACHINE AND
SPACECRAFT FROM
DOCTOR WHO.
PHOTOGRAPHED
BY GUY BELL AT
LONDON FILM AND
COMIC CON 2014.

OPPOSITE TWINS KYLE (LEFT) AND DAVID BIRD POSE WITH THEIR FRIEND JO AS ROAD WARRIORS FROM THE DYSTOPIAN AUSTRALIAN WASTELAND FEATURED IN MAD MAX: THE ROAD WARRIOR. PHOTOGRAPHED BY GUY BELL AT LONDON FILM AND COMIC CON.

RIGHT WITH BIG SHOULDERPADS AND BIGGER HAIR, KERRI NUGENT POSES AS AUNTY ENTITY FROM MAD MAX BEYOND THUNDERDOME. PHOTOGRAPHED AT NEW YORK COMIC CON BY NEILSON BARNARD.

VIDEO GAME HEROES AND HEROINES

PARIS SINCLAIR IS BEAUTIFUL AND DEADLY
IN METALLIC GREEN AS JADE FROM
MORTAL KOMBAT. PHOTOGRAPHED AT
ANIME EXPO 2012 BY MARTIN WONG.

Dressing up as a butt-kicking hero or heroine is the ultimate power fantasy. It's no wonder that cosplay inspired by video games is incredibly popular. Cosplayers have tackled building replicas of characters from nostalgic arcade classics, brutal first-person shooters and even epic role-playing games.

Video-game heroes have very dynamic backstories, motivations and goals – all designed to keep a gamer's attention through hours and hours of game-play. And after spending so many hours playing a particular role in a game, some cosplayers want to continue to explore that character's persona in real life as well as on the screen.

Renee Michelle Gloger is one such cosplayer. She spent hours playing through the *Mass Effect* series of video games, a role-playing first-person shooter in which a gamer will encounter friends and foes from a variety of extraterrestrial origins. Gloger quickly decided that her favourite character was Garrus, a charismatic teammate and potential romantic mate. Since Garrus is a Turian, an alien that looks a bit like a mix between a crab and a cat, Gloger found it was one of her most difficult cosplays, but worth it because of her affection for the character.

"It was something totally outside of my comfort zone and I'm really proud of how it turned out," she says. "It was also really fun transforming my appearance way more than usual by wearing a mask, creating a bodysuit with alien proportions, and then wearing armour on top. He's also my favourite character from one of my favourite video games, so it meant a lot to me to make the costume. Plus wearing it with other friends who like *Mass Effect* – and making new friends through *Mass Effect* photo shoots at cons – makes it even more memorable."

Gogler's most labour-intensive cosplay yet, Garrus took nine months from early start to rapid finish in her hotel room at Dragon*Con, where she was scheduled to wear it. She created a mask of Garrus's alien face by casting it in plastic.

Built for combat, Garrus wears a full armoured suit and frequently wields a gun – a level of heavy armament that is the norm in video games. Perhaps because so many characters are skilled in weaponry, the cosplayers portraying them often wield sophisticated props. Though typically made of light materials that are easy to carry and hardly deadly, the weaponry featured in this book certainly looks impressive enough to kill.

Armed from head to toe in his Deathlord Draugr mail, Bill Doran cuts an imposing figure. Light glints off the detailed swirls decorating his armour, and two LED lights glow from the eyeholes in his horned helm. However, what might not be apparent from his Hollywood-quality armour is that the cosplayer creates every piece from scratch.

Doran and his wife, Brittany, are featured in this book in their Skyrim cosplay armour modelled out of Ethylene-vinyl acetate (EVA) foam, purchased at the local craft store. There is actually no metal on either suit of armour, just a great deal of lightweight foam painted to look metallic. Doran's hobby has turned from a pastime into a full-blown career, in which he builds custom props and sells blueprints of his creations to other cosplayers.

"A high-quality replica prop build can take anywhere from a couple of weeks to several months to build," says Doran. "The construction times can quickly get into the hundreds or thousands of hours. I like to use materials like MDF wood, plastics like PVC and styrene, epoxy clays and a variety of foams to create the master parts for my prop replicas. Once they are finished, they usually get moulded in silicone and cast from urethane plastic."

From guns to swords to staves to armour and prosthetic body parts, props that can make or break a cosplay's accuracy tend to stretch the player's abilities to their very limits. Cosplayer Chaka Cumberbatch says that she's developed an arsenal of skills she'd never had before simply through her hobby of cosplaying.

"I couldn't even stitch a button before I started this hobby. I couldn't paint anything to save my life, had no real grasp of the concept of primer, would probably have never owned a hand sander or a heat gun – which are now two things I can't picture my life without – if it wasn't for cosplay," she says. "That's one of the biggest reasons why I love this hobby and this subculture so much. In my real life, I'm a super-girly girl who is never seen without lipstick or lashes, but when I'm working on cosplay it's like I'm the Home Depot Martha Stewart or something. It's insane how much you learn."

Nobody will deny that cosplay is a lot of effort, so what makes it worth it? For Kara, who goes by the name of Electric Lady in the cosplay world, video-game cosplay gave her an opportunity to meet a voice actor who worked on the game. Dressed as Elizabeth from *BioShock Infinite*, Kara caught the attention of the game's lead voice actor while she was attending a New Mexico fandom convention as a cosplay guest. Since Elizabeth is the companion of the game's lead, her costume provided an opportune icebreaker to meeting one of her heroes.

"Troy Baker, the voice of Booker, was also a guest at the con, and we had fun joking around and throwing coins at each other," she says. "It was a costume I really enjoyed wearing, and I hope to make some of Elizabeth's other outfits at some point as well."

In this chapter, we've featured cosplayers portraying some of the video-game world's most interesting, iconic and deadly denizens. Whenever you see a prop, try to guess what it's made out of, how long it took and how you might go about making it yourself.

LEFT RYAN SMALL PLAYS ALTAIR, A HERO ON A QUEST FOR REDEMPTION IN THE GAME ASSASSIN'S CREED. PHOTOGRAPHED BY GUY BELL AT LONDON FILM AND COMIC CON 2014.

LEFT IN SIGNATURE
BLUE AND YELLOW,
JINRI PARK LOOKS
THE PART OF
STREET FIGHTER'S
BRAWLER CHUN LI.
PHOTOGRAPHED BY
JASON TABLANTE IN
MANILA, PHILIPPINES.

VIDEO GAME HEROES AND HEROINES 125

ABOVE AND OPPOSITE WITH DRAPING FABRIC
AND A SWIRLING MOTIF ON HER CORSET
AND BOOTS, YAYA HAN'S CHUN LI COSTUME
IS INSPIRED BY DECIDEDLY ART NOUVEAU
FAN ART BY KIM RAZVAN. PHOTOGRAPHED IN
ATLANTA, GEORGIA BY BENNY LEE.

126 VIDEO GAME HEROES AND HEROINES

ABOVE ROCHELLE ANNE'S FANS AREN'T JUST FOR SHOW. THEY DOUBLE AS FAKE WEAPONS IN HER COSPLAY AS KITANA FROM MORTAL KOMBAT. PHOTOGRAPHED AT ANIME EXPO 2012 BY MARTIN WONG.

RIGHT RAUL PORRAS OF LEGION6070 COSPLAY LUNGES FOR THE KILL AS RAIDEN FROM MORTAL KOMBAT. PHOTOGRAPHED BY LONG THAI AT COMICPALOOZA 2014.

BELOW CLAD IN CRIMSON, KASEA CIPORKIN IS THE FEROCIOUS SKARLET FROM MORTAL KOMBAT. PHOTOGRAPHED AT ANIME EXPO 2012 BY MARTIN WONG.

ABOVE DEANNA DAVIS, KNOWN IN THE COSPLAY WORLD AS IT'S RAINING NEON, SHOWS OFF HER SKILFUL ARMOUR CONSTRUCTION AS ATHENA FROM BORDERLANDS: THE PRE-SEQUEL. PHOTOGRAPHED AT NEW YORK COMIC CON 2014 BY NICOLE CIARAMELLA.

OPPOSITE MONIKA LEE IS READY TO FACE DANGER IN FULL ARMOUR AS A DEMON HUNTER FROM DIABLO III. PHOTOGRAPHED AT DRAGON CON 2014 BY NICOLE CIARAMELLA.

OPPOSITE ANCIENT RUNES AND A GEM-TIPPED SWORD COMPLETE THE LOOK FOR LUNO AS OSWALD, THE SHADOW KNIGHT OF RPG ODIN'S SPHERE. PHOTOGRAPHED BY ALENA PUGOFFKA.

BELOW SMOKEY EYES AND A PURPLE POUT ADD SULTRY DETAIL TO JULI ABENE'S COSPLAY AS THE SUCCUBUS TEMPTRESS MORRIGAN FROM DARKSTALKERS. PHOTOGRAPHED AT PAX EAST 2014 BY NICOLE CIARAMELLA.

ABOVE TINA LAM, ALSO KNOWN AS TURN ON RED, IS MASKED AND GALLANT AS THE BRAVE BUT BETRAYED CORVO FROM DISHONORED. PHOTOGRAPHED IN MORRIS PLAINS, NEW JERSEY BY NICOLE CIARAMELLA.

OPPOSITE HAYLEY WILLIAMS WOVE GOLDEN EXTENSIONS INTO HER HAIR TO EMULATE STREET FIGHTER CAMMY'S THIGH-LENGTH BRAIDS. PHOTOGRAPHED BY MARTIN WONG AT ANIME EXPO.

RIGHT CATHERINE LEWIS OF GOD SAVE THE QUEEN FASHIONS IS READY TO RUMBLE AS SAKURA FROM STREET FIGHTER. PHOTOGRAPHED BY LONG THAI AT ANIME MATSURI 2014 IN HOUSTON, TEXAS.

BELOW TAKING AIM, AZRIEL GRIMM IS IN CHARACTER AS EDWARD KENWAY OF ASSASSIN'S CREED. GRIMM IS ALSO A MEMBER OF THE ASSASINS COSPLAY BROTHERHOOD. PHOTOGRAPHED BY GUY BELL AT LONDON FILM AND COMIC CON.

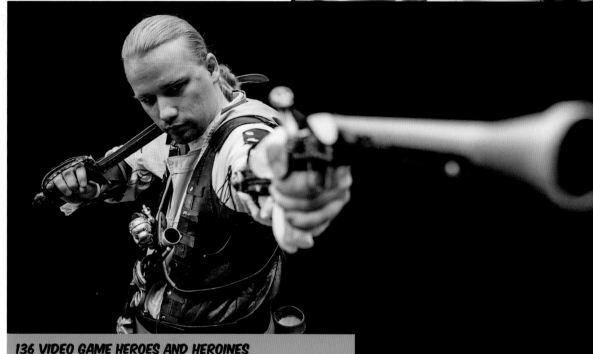

RIGHT BLUE PAINT, FACIAL PROSTHETICS, AND NO SMALL AMOUNT OF CUSTOM ARMOUR TRANSFORM RANA MCANEAR INTO SAMARA, A MEMBER OF THE ASARI RACE IN MASS EFFECT. MCANEAR DOESN'T ONLY COSPLAY AS SAMARA BUT IS THE ORIGINAL FACE MODEL FOR THE VIDEO GAME CHARACTER. PHOTOGRAPHED AT NEW YORK COMIC CON BY MIKE KOWALEK.

OPPOSITE TEXTURED FOAM GIVES CRYSTAL PANDA'S FUTURISTIC ARMOUR ADDITIONAL AUTHENTICITY AS SHE COSPLAYS COMMANDER SHEPARD FROM MASS EFFECT 2. PHOTOGRAPHED AT KATSUCON IN WASHINGTON, DC BY SMIKE KOWALEK.

LEFT AND OPPOSITE
METALLIC DETAILS AND A
SHOCK OF WHITE HAIR
MAKE MELTEM AKCAM'S
COSPLAY A DECIDEDLY
ORIGINAL PORTRAYAL
OF AN ADJUTANT
FROM STARCRAFT.
PHOTOGRAPHED BY
ALTUG ISLER.

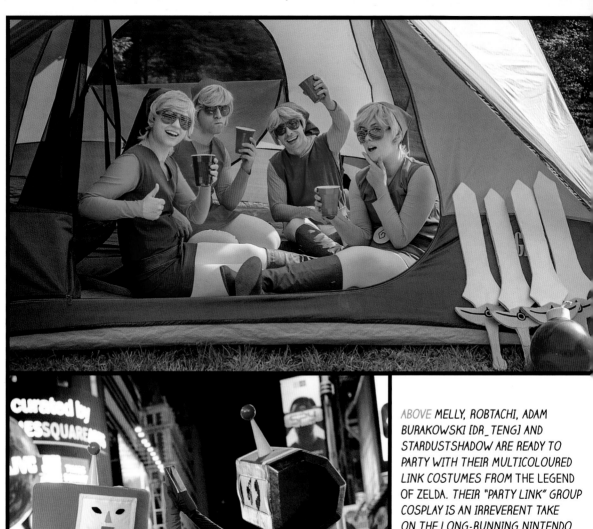

ABOVE MELLY, ROBTACHI, ADAM BURAKOWSKI [DR_TENG] AND STARDUSTSHADOW ARE READY TO PARTY WITH THEIR MULTICOLOURED LINK COSTUMES FROM THE LEGEND OF ZELDA. THEIR "PARTY LINK" GROUP COSPLAY IS AN IRREVERENT TAKE ON THE LONG-RUNNING NINTENDO SERIES. PHOTOGRAPHED BY NICOLE CIARAMELLA.

LEFT SCAPEGOATED (LEFT) AND MAISHERI HAVE A SURREAL MOMENT AS MISO AND MAG – TWO ALIEN CREATURES FROM KATAMARI DAMACY – IN THE MIDDLE OF NEW YORK CITY'S TIMES SQUARE. PHOTOGRAPHED BY MIKE KOWALEK.

OPPOSITE IT'S RAINING NEON IS MAD MOXXI, THE SADISTIC AND ALLURING ANNOUNCER FROM BORDERLANDS. PHOTOGRAPHED BY ANNA FISCHER.

CAMERA TRICKERY PUTS CHRYSS YEN
IN THE GAME AS SHE CHANNELS
FAITH CONNOR FROM MIRROR'S EDGE.
PHOTOGRAPHED IN ATLANTA, GEORGIA BY
BENNY LEE.

BELOW LEELEETHEBUNNY IS READY TO WREAK MAYHEM AS JINX, THE IMPULSIVE TRICKSTER OF LEAGUE OF LEGENDS. HER SHARK-SHAPED ROCKET LAUNCHER SHOWS SHE MEANS BUSINESS. PHOTOGRAPHED AT KATSUCON 2014 BY NICOLE CIARAMELLA.

OPPOSITE ABOVE MRDUSTINN STRIKES A POSE AS A MALE VERSION OF FATE/STAY NIGHT'S SWASHBUCKLING HEROINE SABER. PHOTOGRAPHED BY ERIC NG.

OPPOSITE BELOW WEARING A PERFECTLY TOUSLED WIG, MALINDACHAN MAKES A DASHING LINK FROM LEGEND OF ZELDA: SKYWARD SWORD. PHOTOGRAPHED BY JOSEPH CHI LIN.

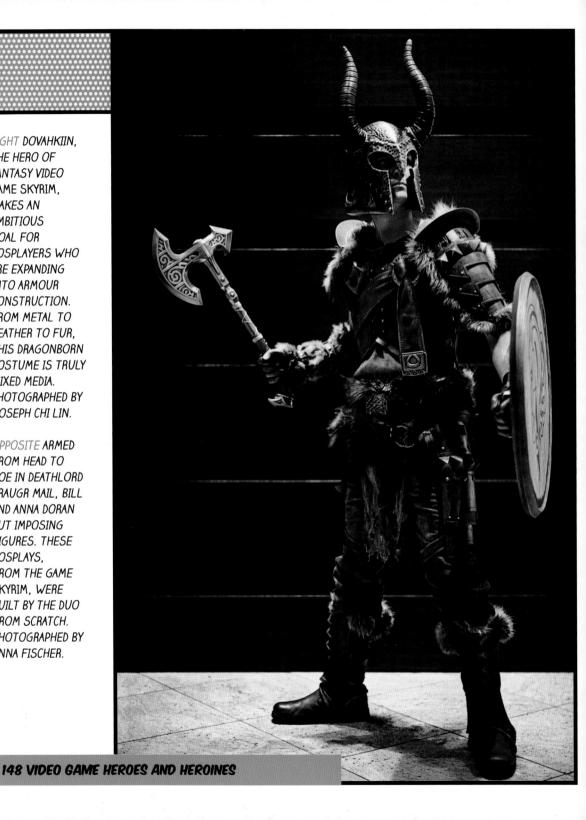

RIGHT DOVAHKIIN, THE HERO OF FANTASY VIDEO GAME SKYRIM, MAKES AN AMBITIOUS GOAL FOR COSPLAYERS WHO ARE EXPANDING INTO ARMOUR CONSTRUCTION. FROM METAL TO LEATHER TO FUR, THIS DRAGONBORN COSTUME IS TRULY MIXED MEDIA. PHOTOGRAPHED BY JOSEPH CHI LIN.

OPPOSITE ARMED FROM HEAD TO TOE IN DEATHLORD DRAUGR MAIL, BILL AND ANNA DORAN CUT IMPOSING FIGURES. THESE COSPLAYS, FROM THE GAME SKYRIM, WERE BUILT BY THE DUO FROM SCRATCH. PHOTOGRAPHED BY ANNA FISCHER.

OPPOSITE *AKI YU, KNOWN BY HER COSPLAY MONIKER POODOKI, DONS A HOODED, IRIDESCENT SUIT OF ARMOUR AS THE STEALTHY DEMON HUNTER FROM DIABLO. PHOTOGRAPHED AT ANIME EXPO IN LOS ANGELES, CALIFORNIA BY MIKE KOWALEK.*

BELOW *IN A SWIRLING CAPE, KIMMY BRANDISHES HER SWORD AS LUCINA FROM FIRE EMBLEM. PHOTOGRAPHED AT OTAKON 2014 BY NICOLE CIARAMELLA.*

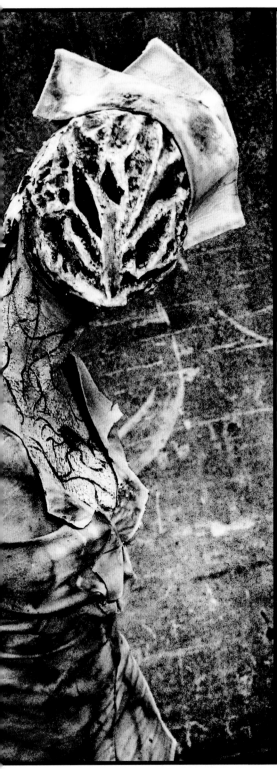

LEFT ASHGROOVY (LEFT) AND VOXTHEFOX ARE THE GRISLY PYRAMID HEAD AND A TWISTED NURSE FROM THE SILENT HILL HORROR GAME FRANCHISE. PHOTOGRAPHED BY JUDITH STEPHENS.

ABOVE THIS LONDON FILM AND COMIC CON REVELLER BALANCES FORMIDABLE HORNS AS ULTIMECIA FROM FINAL FANTASY VIII. PHOTOGRAPHED BY GUY BELL.

OPPOSITE KAIEN YUU IS A BATTLE-READY LIGHTNING FROM FINAL FANTASY XIII. SPECIAL EFFECTS LEND CREDENCE TO LIGHTNING'S POWERFUL ENERGY. PHOTOGRAPHED BY MICHAEL OOI.

BELOW ACE'S REI, EVA, ANDREW LIEW, REGHEG YOK, CORVER LIM, TA KA YUKI, YVONNE CHIAH ELF AND CHIAKI CHEN ASSEMBLE TO PORTRAY EVERY PLAYABLE CHARACTER IN FINAL FANTASY XIII. PHOTOGRAPHED BY MICHAEL OOI.

OVERLEAF ALTHAIR INFLESH DEFENDS THE IMPERIAL CULT AS A MINISTORUM PRIEST FROM THE GAME WARHAMMER 40,000. THE VIDEO GAME IS BASED ON A TABLETOP GAME WHERE PLAYERS BATTLE WITH FIGURES THAT RESEMBLE FANTASY CHARACTERS. PHOTOGRAPHED BY ALENA PUGOFFKA.

ABOVE A STAINED GLASS WINDOW
PROVIDES DRAMATIC LIGHTING TO
THESE STARKLY POSED BOOKER
AND ELIZABETH COSPLAYERS FROM
BIOSHOCK INFINITE. PHOTOGRAPHED BY
ALENA PUGOFFKA.

OPPOSITE JUDSON, KEVIN, LAURA,
SARAH, SHELBY, ZACH AND GAVIN
MAKE A GRIM FAMILY PORTRAIT POSED
AS VARIOUS ANTAGONISTS FROM
BIOSHOCK. PHOTOGRAPHED IN ATLANTA,
GEORGIA BY BENNY LEE.

ABOVE VICTORY ROLLS AND NAUTICAL
STRIPING MAKE A PATRIOTIC '50S COSTUME
FOR ALEX ABENE AS ELIZABETH FROM
BIOSHOCK INFINITE: BURIAL AT SEA.
PHOTOGRAPHED AT PAX EAST 2014 BY NICOLE
CIARAMELLA.

RIGHT STUNNING AFTER-EFFECTS PAINT
A TABLEAU OF LIGHT AROUND KARA, ALSO
KNOWN AS ELECTRIC LADY, COSPLAYING HERE
AS ELIZABETH FROM BIOSHOCK INFINITE.
"BIOSHOCK IS ONE OF MY FAVOURITE GAME
SERIES, I LOVE THE SETTINGS, THE CONCEPT,
AND INFINITE WAS AN AMAZING TIE-IN TO THE
ORIGINAL RAPTURE," SHE SAYS. "I ORIGINALLY
MADE THE COSTUME FOR WORK TO WEAR
AT THE MIDNIGHT LAUNCH FOR THE GAME. I
HAD ABOUT A WEEK AND A HALF TO FINISH!"
PHOTOGRAPHED BY MARTIN WONG AT FANIME.

LEFT MAKI ROLL IS BLACKROSE, THE TOUGH BUT LOYAL PROTAGONIST FROM THE .HACK SERIES OF GAMES. PHOTOGRAPHED BY ANNA FISCHER.

OPPOSITE WITH THE HELP OF CONTOURED BLUE BODY PAINT AND NO SMALL NUMBER OF FACIAL PROSTHETICS, KUDREL COSPLAY IS DOWNRIGHT FERAL AS A TROLL SHAMAN FROM WORLD OF WARCRAFT. PHOTOGRAPHED AT KATSUCON 2013 BY JUDITH STEPHENS.

RIGHT WIELDING A HAND-PAINTED STAFF, YIVON POSES AS A PETITE ELIN PRIEST FROM THE SOUTH KOREAN MASSIVELY MULTIPLAYER ONLINE GAME TERA ONLINE. "THE ENTIRE COSTUME WAS MADE BY MYSELF, EXCEPT FOR THE WIG OF COURSE. THE COSTUME IS MADE WITH WHITE BROCADE CLOTH AND PURPLE VELVETEEN FOR THE OUTER COAT. I HAD THESE MATERIALS IMPORTED, AS IT'S REALLY PRICEY TO GET IT LOCALLY. THE FURRY EARS AND TAIL WERE REALLY FUN TO MAKE. I ONLY HAD TWO FUR COLOURS WITH ME, WHITE AND ORANGE, SO I HAD TO COLOUR SOME PARTS OF THE FUR TO MAKE THEM LOOK BETTER," SHE SAYS. PHOTOGRAPHED BY THOMAS KUAN AT COSFEST XIII, A FANDOM CONVENTION IN SINGAPORE.

OPPOSITE NINE TAILS POISED, CHRISTY KIM IS AHRI, A MAGICAL FOX WITH STRONG SPIRITUAL POWER IN THE LEAGUE OF LEGENDS UNIVERSE. PHOTOGRAPHED IN ATLANTA, GEORGIA BY BENNY LEE.

ABOVE GIN USES SPECIAL EFFECTS
MAKEUP AND ARMOUR-PIERCING
ARROW PROPS TO PORTRAY A
PARTICULARLY DIFFICULT DAY FOR
ELVEN WARRIOR FENRIS FROM
DRAGON AGE. PHOTOGRAPHED IN
MOSCOW BY ALENA PUGOFFKA.

OPPOSITE BOOMIE OF STRAWBERRY
CENSOR COSPLAY WIELDS AN AXE
AS BIG AS HERSELF AS A PART
OF HER BLADE & SOUL COSPLAY.
PHOTOGRAPHED BY ERIC NG.

168 VIDEO GAME HEROES AND HEROINES

OPPOSITE MOTLEY FABRIC CHOICES AND GEISHA HAIR ACCESSORIES ADD FLAIR TO YURKARY'S PORTRAYAL OF MIFUYU, A JAPANESE CHARACTER FROM THE ONLINE GAME GRANADO ESPADA. PHOTOGRAPHED BY THOMAS KUAN.

ABOVE TINA, ALSO KNOWN AS TURN ON RED, PERSONIFIES THE ECCENTRIC MERCHANT RAVIO FROM THE LEGEND OF ZELDA: A LINK BETWEEN WORLDS. PHOTOGRAPHED AT PAX EAST 2014 BY NICOLE CIARAMELLA.

OPPOSITE NICOLE CIARAMELLA WHIRLS HER CAPE AS THARJA FROM FIRE EMBLEM. PHOTOGRAPHED BY JUDITH STEPHENS.

RIGHT RIDDLE'S MESSY WARDROBE POSES AS MASTER ARCHER ASHE FROM LEAGUE OF LEGENDS. PHOTOGRAPHED BY JUDITH STEPHENS.

RIGHT CUSTOM SHADES ADD A
FUTURISTIC FEEL TO CRISTINA GÓMEZ
(LEFT), UMISTER AND MELLY'S TEAM
FLARE COSPLAY FROM POKÉMON. THE
THREE CHANNEL THE ICONIC VILLAINS IN
BRIGHT RED APPAREL, NEON WIGS AND
LIPSTICK TO MATCH. PHOTOGRAPHED
AT DRAGON CON 2014 BY NICOLE
CIARAMELLA.

TV ICONS AND POP CULTURE PINUPS

IN RENAISSANCE ERA FINERY THAT WOULD
NOT HAVE BEEN OUT OF PLACE IN 1492
ITALY, DIA (LEFT), UMISTER AND MELLY
ARE THE BORGIAS, THE HISTORICAL
CRIME FAMILY FEATURED IN THE
SHOWTIME SERIES OF THE SAME NAME.
PHOTOGRAPHED AT DRAGONCON 2014 BY
JUDITH STEPHENS.

You'd expect to see Batman at a comics convention. But you might be a little surprised if he was joined by Robin Hood, Princess Jasmine and Frodo. However, we've found and featured cosplays of all three of those characters at conventions far and wide.

As cosplay becomes more popular, it's not just fans of lesser-known science fiction and anime shows who have taken part in the fun. Now you can find cosplay of any beloved character in any realm of pop culture.

Pop-culture costume inspiration usually comes from any TV series or film that has reached mainstream popularity, but it can also originate from public figures such as pop stars – Lady Gaga's avant-garde sartorial choices are an especial favourite with cosplayers.

There's an irreverence in pop-culture cosplay, a sense of playfulness that occurs with mainstream costumes to a greater extent than with more niche fantasy outfits. Perhaps it's because people remember seeing their favourite costumed characters at Disneyland and the childlike joy inherent in that. Adam Burakowski, who also goes under the name of Dr_Teng in the cosplay world, is clear that there's a difference depending on costume. "The laughs I get out of wearing Zapp Brannigan are a lot different than the satisfaction I get out of wearing a Superman costume," he says.

While most cosplays focus on imitating a character, pop culture costumes are often subject to vigorous personalization. Since these characters are so well known, cosplayers can easily conduct heavy costume customizations while still being recognizable.

For example, instead of dressing as Doctor Who, a cosplayer might make a TARDIS-inspired ball gown. And it's Twilight Sparkle's variegated hair and unicorn horn that make her recognizable, not her hooves – leading to a slew of *My Little Pony: Friendship is Magic* cosplayers creating distinctly human but still identifiable pony cosplays. There's also an entire genre called "casual cosplay", in which cosplayers attempt to create still-recognizable cosplays using almost entirely regular store-bought clothing for materials.

It's the clothes and the hairstyle that make a pop culture cosplay discernable, not trivial things like, say, the gender of the cosplayer wearing it. In fact, today, cosplaying outside of one's gender has become so common, there's even a term for it: crossplay. Whether it's a masculine take on a Disney Prince, a feminine version of Aqua Girl, or even a male cosplayer in an original ball gown, anything goes.

The same goes for ethnicity. Mari-chan, the pseudonym of an African American cosplayer, said it was the cosplay community's acceptance that has encouraged her to portray her favourite characters, regardless of their skin tones on TV.

"At first I was very hesitant to cosplay Princess Serenity [from *Sailor Moon*]," she says. "I'm a bit of a perfectionist, so there was that part of me that said, 'If I cosplay outside of my skin tone, it won't look right.' But I was shocked by the love and support it received."

The clearest example of the community's unified acceptance occurred when worldwide clothing brand Hot Topic created a shirt that said, "Cosplay: Do it right or not at all." For the modern cosplayer, this goes completely against the idea that cosplay is for everyone, whether they buy their outfits or sew them from scratch, whatever their body shape of skin tone.

Cosplayers quickly let Hot Topic know that they didn't accept the definition the company used to define their community. As cosplay gets more and more popular, cosplayers are stressing you don't have to have a certain body to dress like your favourite character. In the end, Hot Topic was simply forced to bow to the outcry and withdraw the shirt from sale.

There are a lot of different ways to do pop culture inspired cosplay "right", and the measure of success is less of a reaction than a feeling. For cosplayer Chaka Cumberbatch, that means sticking to cosplaying characters she adores and feels good personifying, regardless of peer pressure.

"I'll have friends ask me to join random cosplay groups, just to help fill out the roster or because they think I'd really work for a particular character, and I almost always politely decline because for me, it's hard to get in the zone of creating a costume for a character you don't feel any particular pull towards," she says.

"If it's a character you love, it doesn't feel so much like work. It feels more like bringing a dream to life – and that feeling is important, because you need it to push you through all the moments of frustration and mistakes and bobbins that refuse to thread."

In this chapter, you'll see cosplayers from all over the world impersonating some of their favourite pop culture icons. For Singaporean cosplayer Peggy Sim, that means Japanese mega idol Kyary Pamyu Pamyu, though Western fans may not have heard of her. For Hungary's Tu ba Erma, it means channeling timeless seductress Betty Boop. And for no small number of American and European fans, it means TV characters like the full cast of hit fantasy series *Game of Thrones*. Whether exacting recreations or creative homages, you're bound to recognize plenty of these pop culture icons.

LEFT IN A PSYCHEDELIC DRESS DOTTED WITH QUIRKY DETAILS, PEGGY SIM PORTRAYS CUTESY JAPANESE POPSTAR KYARY PAMYU PAMYU. PHOTOGRAPHED BY THOMAS KUAN.

LEFT MORE THAN 250 BUTTONS, GEMS AND PEARLS ARE SEWN INTO ALYSSA'S COSPLAY AS CORA, QUEEN OF HEARTS FROM THE FAIRYTALE-INSPIRED TV SHOW ONCE UPON A TIME. ALYSSA IS ONE HALF OF THE COSPLAY DUO PROPPED UP CREATIONS, KNOWN FOR MAKING DETAILED TUTORIALS OF EACH COSTUME THEY CREATE. PHOTOGRAPHED AT CABINCON 2014 BY JUDITH STEPHENS.

ABOVE *WOLFIE IS IN A TIGHT SPOT AS FLYNN RIDER FROM DISNEY'S TANGLED. PHOTOGRAPHED AT ANIME USA 2011 BY NICOLE CIARAMELLA.*

OPPOSITE *SOME TRICKY LIGHTING AND SPECIAL EFFECTS TRANSFORM ALEXIS INTO A DIMINUTIVE THUMBELINA. PHOTOGRAPHED IN DULUTH, GEORGIA, BY BENNY LEE.*

OPPOSITE AND RIGHT
RESPLENDENT IN
GOLDEN LAYERS, THIS
BELLE COSPLAYER IS
THE BELLE OF LONDON
FILM AND COMIC CON
2014. PHOTOGRAPHED
BY GUY BELL.

IN COZY MITTENS
AND SCANDINAVIAN
EMBROIDERY, HELENA
EVANS IS PRINCESS
ANNA FROM FROZEN.
PHOTOGRAPHED BY ALENA
PUGOFFKA IN MOSCOW.

LEFT MILENA HIME'S HANDCRAFTED FEATHERED HEADDRESS AND GOLDEN BROCADE GOWN TRANSFORM HER INTO THE TOOTH FAIRY FROM RISE OF THE GUARDIANS. PHOTOGRAPHED BY ALENA PUGOFFKA IN MOSCOW.

ABOVE A TOOTHSOME SMILE AND FUZZY STRIPES MAKE FOR AN ARRESTING AND DETAILED CHESHIRE CAT FROM ALICE'S ADVENTURES IN WONDERLAND. BELIEVE IT OR NOT, EMPRESS OF SQUEE STARTED WITH A SQUARE BLOCK OF FOAM ADHESIVE IN ORDER TO CARVE THIS EXPRESSIVE FACE! EACH TOOTH WAS INDIVIDUALLY SCULPTED OUT OF CLAY AND DIPPED IN GLOW-IN-THE-DARK PAINT. PHOTOGRAPHED AT OTAKUTHON IN MONTREAL, CANADA BY MIKE KOWALEK.

OPPOSITE A GNARLED STAFF MAKES A DRAMATIC CONTRAST TO MAMORU'S ELEGANT BROCADE JACKET AS HE POSES AS JACK FROST FROM RISE OF THE GUARDIANS. PHOTOGRAPHED BY ALENA PUGOFFKA IN MOSCOW.

LEFT NEGATIVINFINITY'S HISTORICALLY ACCURATE SNOW WHITE COSPLAY IS INSPIRED BY ILLUSTRATOR CLAIRE HUMMEL'S RENDITION OF HOW THE DISNEY PRINCESS WOULD HAVE LOOKED IN HER ORIGINAL TIME PERIOD OF 1500-1530. PHOTOGRAPHED BY JUDITH STEPHENS AT CABINCON 2014.

OPPOSITE MELTINGMIRROR SEETHES WITH LUXURY AND CRUELTY AS CRUELLA DE VIL FROM DISNEY'S ONE HUNDRED AND ONE DALMATIANS. PHOTOGRAPHED AT COSTUME-CON IN TORONTO, CANADA BY MIKE KOWALEK.

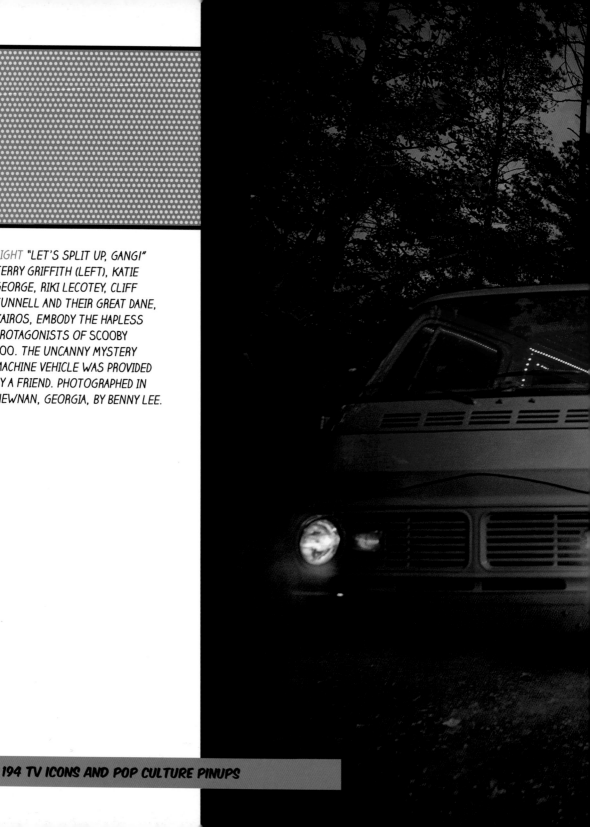

RIGHT *"LET'S SPLIT UP, GANG!"*
JERRY GRIFFITH (LEFT), KATIE
GEORGE, RIKI LECOTEY, CLIFF
TUNNELL AND THEIR GREAT DANE,
KAIROS, EMBODY THE HAPLESS
PROTAGONISTS OF SCOOBY
DOO. THE UNCANNY MYSTERY
MACHINE VEHICLE WAS PROVIDED
BY A FRIEND. PHOTOGRAPHED IN
NEWNAN, GEORGIA, BY BENNY LEE.

RIGHT HAND-DRAWN DETAILS MAKE THE DIFFERENCE IN TONY PRIME'S OPTIMUS PRIME ARMOUR. THE SINGAPOREAN IS BEST KNOWN FOR HIS PLATEMAIL CREATIONS. PHOTOGRAPHED BY THOMAS KUAN.

OPPOSITE THERE'S NO PHOTOSHOP TRICKERY IN YAYA HAN'S IMPOSSIBLE MEASUREMENTS AS CARTOON BOMBSHELL JESSICA RABBIT. THE INNOVATIVE COSPLAYER BUILT A STEEL-BONE CORSET AND TWO PADDED BRAS INTO HER SLINKY SEQUIN GOWN. PHOTOGRAPHED BY ANNA FISCHER.

LEFT A SMOKY ATMOSPHERE ENHANCES LINDZE MERRITT'S GHASTLY PALLOR AS MALEFICENT FROM SLEEPING BEAUTY. PHOTOGRAPHED IN ATLANTA, GEORGIA, BY BENNY LEE.

BELOW BETH MALCOLM PUTS
A MORE MODERN SPIN ON
THE VILLAINOUS MALEFICENT,
CHOOSING TO PORTRAY ANGELINA
JOLIE'S CHARACTER FROM THE
2014 FILM RATHER THAN THE 1959
ANIMATION. PHOTOGRAPHED AT
LONDON FILM AND COMIC CON BY
GUY BELL.

OPPOSITE ROBIN HOOD AND
LITTLE JOHN AS PORTRAYED
BY HUSBAND-AND-WIFE
COSPLAYERS SENSEE AND SONER.
PHOTOGRAPHED BY ALTUG ISLER.

LEFT IT MAY LOOK LIKE SCOUT ISENSEE (LEFT) AND JENNIFER DE CABRERA [BOMBAYCAKE] HAVE TRAVELLED TO MIDDLE EARTH FOR THEIR FRODO AND SAM FROM LORD OF THE RINGS COSPLAY, BUT PHOTOGRAPHER NICOLE CIARAMELLA INSISTS THAT THIS IS JUST A PARTICULARLY WOODED AREA OF CENTRAL PARK, NEW YORK CITY.

BELOW IN ELVEN FINERY AND TWIG FASCINATORS, TWO COSPLAYERS PORTRAY ELROND AND HIS TWIN BROTHER ELROS AT LONDON FILM AND COMIC CON. PHOTOGRAPHED BY GUY BELL.

RIGHT METALLIC PAINT TRANSFORMS
COMIC CON ATTENDEE CHRISTOPHER
HALL INTO WAR MACHINE FROM THE
IRON MAN *SERIES*. PHOTOGRAPHED AT
NEW YORK COMIC CON BY NEILSON
BARNARD.

LEFT A FULL PLASTIC SUIT TRANSFORMS CHARLES POYNTER, AKA CHAKS PRODUCTIONS, INTO A LIFE-SIZED LEGO MAN AS EMMET BRICKOWSKI FROM THE LEGO MOVIE. PHOTOGRAPHED BY LONG THAI AT DALLAS COMIC-CON 2014.

OPPOSITE IT TAKES DEDICATION TO THE CRAFT TO WALK AROUND ALL DAY IN A LEGO SUIT, AS THIS EMMET BRICKOWSKI COSPLAYER DID AT LONDON FILM AND COMIC CON. PHOTOGRAPHED BY GUY BELL.

ABOVE WHO YOU GONNA CALL? WHY NOT TRY THIS TEAM OF INTREPID GHOSTBUSTERS, ARMED AND READY IN THEIR JUMPSUITS AND PROTON PACKS. PHOTOGRAPHED AT PAX EAST 2014 BY NICOLE CIARAMELLA.

OPPOSITE ARMED WITH A PROTON PACK REPLICA, THIS GHOSTBUSTERS COSPLAYER ISN'T AFRAID OF NO GHOST. PHOTOGRAPHED AT NEW YORK COMIC CON BY NEILSON BARNARD.

OPPOSITE SILK FLOWERS AND BUTTERFLY LASHES ADD DECADENT DETAILS TO BREATHLESSAIRE'S COSPLAY AS EFFIE TRINKET FROM THE HUNGER GAMES. PHOTOGRAPHED BY JOSEPH CHI LIN.

BELOW COSPLAY CAN BE A WAY FOR FANS TO REIMAGINE THEIR FAVOURITE STORIES. HERE, WISPERIA AND MAMORU ENVISION AN ALTERNATE ENDING TO THE HARRY POTTER SERIES, IN WHICH LILY AND SNAPE END UP TOGETHER. PHOTOGRAPHED BY ALENA PUGOFFKA IN MOSCOW.

ABOVE *DEAD PIXEL PRINCESS (LEFT)*
AND JESSICA LOOK FITTINGLY ROYAL
AS THE QUEEN'S CARDS FROM ALICE'S
ADVENTURES IN WONDERLAND. *THEIR*
COSTUMES ARE INSPIRED BY THE
JAPANESE ILLUSTRATOR SAKIZOU,
WHO IS KNOWN FOR INVENTING
ELEGANT COSTUME DESIGNS.

OPPOSITE *FROM BEADED BRAIDS TO*
BRACELETS AND AN ELABORATE BELT
BUCKLE, CAPTAIN JACK SPARROW
FROM DISNEY'S PIRATES OF THE
CARIBBEAN *CERTAINLY KNOWS HOW*
TO ACCESSORIZE. PHOTOGRAPHED
BY DANIEL BOCZARSKI AT CHICAGO
COMIC CON.

RIGHT ARMED WITH HER TRADEMARK GOGGLES AND WHIP, MENG AI MAKES A DANGEROUS CATWOMAN. PHOTOGRAPHED AT NEW YORK COMIC CON BY NEILSON BARNARD.

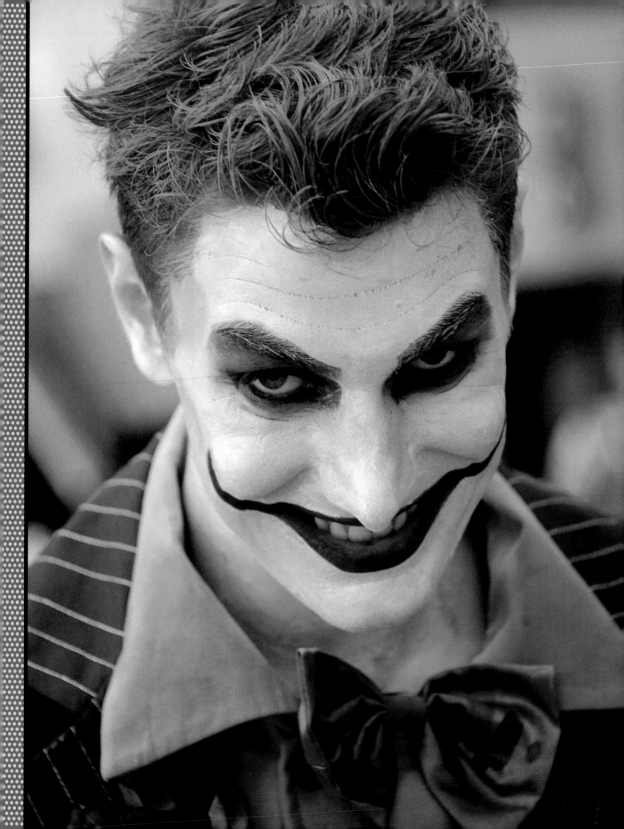

LEFT YOU CAN TELL BY THE GREY LEOTARD AND YELLOW UTILITY BELT THAT THIS IS AN OLD SCHOOL BATMAN COSPLAY FROM THE HERO'S EARLIER ERA.

OPPOSITE WITH A MILE-LONG SNEER, A COSPLAYER CERTAINLY LOOKS THE PART AS THE JOKER FROM BATMAN AT THE THIRD ANNUAL STAN LEE'S COMIKAZE EXPO HELD AT LOS ANGELES CONVENTION CENTER.

RIGHT ALYSSA KING CAUSES MAYHEM AS BATMAN *VILLAIN* HARLEY QUINN WITH HER ENORMOUS HAMMER PROP. PHOTOGRAPHED AT NEW YORK COMIC CON BY NEILSON BARNARD.

OPPOSITE JESS HODGES 29, FROM ROBERTSBRIDGE, POSES AS A CHARACTER FROM THE MUSICAL CATS AHEAD OF THE MCM LONDON COMIC CON EXPO AT EXCEL ON 26 OCTOBER 2012 IN LONDON, ENGLAND. VISITORS TO THE COMIC CONVENTION ARE ENCOURAGED TO WEAR A COSTUME OF THEIR FAVOURITE CHARACTER AND FLOCK TO THE EXPO TO GATHER ALL THE LATEST NEWS IN THE WORLD OF COMICS, MANGA, ANIME, FILM, COSPLAY, GAMES AND CULT FICTION.

ABOVE ERIN SPRADLIN AS ELPHABA AND CHELSEA JOHNSON AS GLINDA LINK ARMS AS THE UNLIKELY FRIENDS FROM THE MUSICAL WICKED. PHOTOGRAPHED BY LONG THAI AT COMICPALOOZA 2014.

OPPOSITE *RESPLENDENT IN FANTASY GETUPS, A GROUP COSPLAYS NEARLY THE FULL GAME OF THRONES CAST AT DRAGONCON 2011. PHOTOGRAPHED BY JUDITH STEPHENS.*

RIGHT *IN A MIX OF FEMININE BROCADE AND BRAWNY LEATHER, MEAGAN MARIE IS BEAUTIFUL AND BRAVE DAENERYS TARGARYEN, MOTHER OF DRAGONS. PHOTOGRAPHED IN NEW MEXICO BY ANNA FISCHER.*

RIGHT ALEXANDRA DITULLIO SWINGS HER CAPE AND SCYTHE AS THE TITULAR CHARACTER OF RWBY, A SUPERNATURAL ANIMATED SHOW. PHOTOGRAPHED AT KATSUCON 2013 BY MARTIN WONG.

CREATIVE COSPLAY: ORIGINAL LOOKS

MOSTFLOGGED, LOVEJOKER, KITSUNE DOLLY AND SEWTHOUGHTFUL EMBODY THE FOUR STICK-FIGURE PROTAGONISTS OF HOMESTUCK IN NEON-BRIGHT "TRICKSTER" RENDITIONS OF THEIR USUAL ATTIRE. PHOTOGRAPHED AT NEW YORK CITY'S DYLAN'S CANDY BAR BY JUDITH STEPHENS.

With hundreds of thousands of characters for cosplayers to choose from, it's no wonder that even the most devoted fans will spot unfamiliar costumes at conventions. However, sometimes the reason you can't identify a cosplay is simply because it is not based on an actual character. These original costumes can be about an aesthetic or style of dress that has barely any relation to everyday clothing worn around the world.

Steampunk is one of these. A genre used for everything from books to films to fan creations, Steampunk imagines a world with technology that far surpasses that of today, but uses nothing more than Victorian-era source materials to create it. As a costume genre, Steampunk takes its cues from Victorian dress, but adds clockwork details and ostensibly steam-powered props. It's not surprising to see Steampunk outfits that resemble those of modern scientists, adventurers and even space explorers. Just read Jules Verne's *20,000 Leagues Under the Sea* or Alan Moore's *The League of Extraordinary Gentlemen* to understand where cosplayers' historic/futuristic inspiration comes from.

Cyberpunk is a modern riff on the same thing – imagining a world in the near future that harnesses nothing more than the power and promise of '90s-era electronics. As a costuming genre, it borrows elements from raver clothing, like glowing neon, glossy black vinyl and metallic blue lipstick. The 90s hit film *The Matrix* and tabletop card game *Netrunner* are premium examples of the Cyberpunk concept.

Other original costuming may not originate from an aesthetic but from a story made famous through global mythologies. Mermaids, fairies and nymphs come straight out of Nordic, pagan and Greek mythology. Today they still inspire seamstresses to take gauzy, wispy materials and floral garlands to create costumes that seem as ethereal as their sources.

Sometimes, original costumes are inspired by actual creatures. Crafters construct outfits and personas around their favourite animals – real ones such as tigers and wolves as well as fictional ones like dragons and unicorns. Costumers that centre their creations specifically around animal suits call themselves furries, a term that refers to the animal nature of their costumes (though some furries choose animals with no fur at all – reptiles, for instance).

Tommy Bruce, a photographer who primarily documents furry fandom, explains the way people who wear anthropomorphic costumes connect with their animal personas. "Fursuits are representations of individuals' fursonas – the furry term for an alternative persona – and are as such extensions of the creator," he says. "This just becomes a little hairier when you factor in people with multiple costumes, or fursuit makers who build their own designed costumes and auction them off. Some consider the purchase of a character designed by another artist to be an 'adoption', the language implying that you aren't just purchasing a piece of art or a costume but a full fictional character with personality and traits."

How do these original costumes fit into the realm of cosplay? Simply in the way that original costumes, just like all other types of cosplay, are about theatrics. A certain amount of play-acting, from trademark poses to a particular speech style, differentiates cosplayers from people just wearing costumes.

However, while cosplayers dressed as a specific character from TV or film would usually say they're performing a tribute to that character, cosplay photographer Anna Fischer believes original costume designers are more likely than their counterparts to assume a specific character persona to go with the outfit they've created.

"Most cosplayers aren't pretending to be the character they're dressed like," she says. "They are performers portraying a character, not people who believe that they've become incarnations of the character once they put on their clothes. The issue of fluidity of identity is more nuanced than transformative in cosplay. Steampunks and furries, however, are more likely to do the whole persona thing, and it's one of the major cultural divides between those communities and other kinds of cosplay."

Assuming a different persona is the ultimate fantasy. With cosplay, you change not only the way others perceive you but, for a little while, how you perceive yourself.

To put an even more complicated spin on what does and does not fall into the boundaries of original costumes, there are also cosplays based on characters that exist but who have never been seen. Fans have only a persona to go on, and their cosplays envision a physical appearance the individual cosplayer has mentally connected with it.

Welcome to *Night Vale*, an online radio show created by Joseph Fink and Jeffrey Cranor, which has an audio-only fandom. Though thousands of fans have listened to the voices of the mysterious Cecil Palmer and his scientist boyfriend Carlos, nobody has any idea what they look like, and cosplayers have a ball trying out their own renditions. In this chapter, cosplayer Frekels envisions Cecil as a not-quite-human creature, with intricate purple tattoos and a central third eye.

Homestuck, created by Andrew Hussie, is another fandom ripe for semi-original cosplays. The canon form is an online comic and interactive game, in which, aside from a few differentiating props like scarves and glasses, fans can only guess at the characters' clothing, ethnicities and true appearances. This has made it extremely popular with cosplayers who are eager to stretch their creative muscles while still creating a recognizable cosplay.

Mermaids, wood nymphs, steampunks, ravers, furries and more fill this chapter with their creative renditions of aesthetics, concepts, myths and personas. In the following pages, you'll see creations that include a mermaid from Hawaii, a mythological goddess from China and cyberpunk ravers that come from the future – or at least have a futuristic resonance.

ABOVE IN HEAD TO TOE BLACK-AND-WHITE STRIPES, TESS MAKES JAILBIRD COUTURE LOOK EDGY AND MODERN. PHOTOGRAPHED AT KATSUCON 2010 BY NICOLE CIARAMELLA.

DRAMATIC FACE MAKEUP AND PLUSH, PRISMATIC HORNS COMPLETE THE LOOK OF LADY EVE'S RAVER CONCOCTION. PHOTOGRAPHED AT KATSUCON 2012 BY NICOLE CIARAMELLA.

OPPOSITE, RIGHT & BELOW DANIELLE LAFLEUR HANDCRAFTED A SALMON-COLOURED MERMAID TAIL FROM WATERPROOF MATERIALS FOR THIS WATERFALL PHOTOSHOOT IN RICKETTS GLEN, PENNSYLVANIA. PHOTOGRAPHED BY NICOLE CIARAMELLA.

LEFT TUBES OF GLOWING NEON SET
YUFFIEBUNNY'S RAVER OUTFIT APART
FROM THE REST. SPIKED SHOULDERS AND
A DRAMATIC NECKLINE COMPLETE HER
ANDROGYNOUS LOOK. "I LOVE BRINGING
MY ORIGINAL DESIGNS TO LIFE, LIKE MY
RAVE COSTUMES," SHE SAYES. "IT GIVES
ME THE CHANCE TO MAKE SOMETHING
THAT'S MORE PERSONAL AND TO
EXPERIMENT WITHOUT THE WORRY OF ANY
KIND OF BOUNDARIES." PHOTOGRAPHED AT
ANIME USA 2013 BY NICOLE CIARAMELLA.

ABOVE HOT PINK HAIR AND BLUE
LIPSTICK SET OFF ANDROID MACHINA'S
MULTICOLOURED DREADLOCKED WIG.
PHOTOGRAPHED AT ANIME USA 2013 BY
NICOLE CIARAMELLA.

LEFT A GROUP OF PEOPLE WEARING MADEFURYOU BRAND FURSUITS POSE FOR A GROUP PHOTO AT MIDWEST FURFEST 2013. IT TAKES MADEFURYOU THREE TO SEVEN DAYS TO BUILD EACH COSTUME FROM SCRATCH. "WE ARE NOT JUST MAKING COSTUMES, BUT CHARACTERS!" THE COMPANY WEBSITE DECLARES. "ONCE YOU PUT ON YOUR COSTUME THE CHARACTER WILL COME ALIVE." PHOTOGRAPHED BY TOMMY BRUCE.

ABOVE TANGO DONS A SUPERMAN OUTFIT
OVER A FOX SUIT AT FURRY WEEKEND
ATLANTA 2014. PHOTOGRAPHED BY
TOMMY BRUCE.

ABOVE WRAPPED IN A FLOWING GOWN THAT ECHOES HER FLOWING HAIR, CHEN YANG DRESSES IN A TRADITIONAL TAKE ON A NATURE GODDESS. PHOTOGRAPHED BY THOMAS KUAN IN SINGAPORE.

RIGHT IN SUMPTUOUS BROCADE AND FUR WITH A FEATHER FASCINATOR TO MATCH, CHEN YANG DONS HER UNIQUE PORTRAYAL OF A FASHIONABLE CHINESE GODDESS. PHOTOGRAPHED BY THOMAS KUAN IN SINGAPORE

RIGHT JUDITH STEPHENS CAPTURES FELLOW COSPLAY PHOTOGRAPHER NICOLE CIARAMELLA (LEFT) AND MELLY IN GOWNS INSPIRED BY BOTH GOTHIC AND NATURAL ELEMENTS.

LEFT *FROM BRIGHT RED TOP HAT TO SHINY VINYL HEEL, KASAHARA GETS FANCY IN HER MOULIN ROUGE-INSPIRED ORIGINAL COSTUME. PHOTOGRAPHED BY ALENA PUGOFFKA.*

OPPOSITE *IN RED-TIPPED HORNS AND KIMONO, LAMPOCHKA DOES HER BEST IMPRESSION OF A GYUKI, A SUPERNATURAL MONSTER OF LEGEND AND MYTH IN JAPAN. PHOTOGRAPHED BY ALENA PUGOFFKA.*

RIGHT ENORMOUS CHRYSANTHEMUMS LEND AN AUTUMNAL FEEL TO CHEN YANG'S ELEGANT ORIGINAL COSTUME. PHOTOGRAPHED BY THOMAS KUAN IN SINGAPORE.

OPPOSITE IRIDESCENT PINK HAIR AND MILE-HIGH BOOTS GIVE JAZZMIN JOLLY A LOOK THAT'S JUST WILD ENOUGH FOR A RAVE. PHOTOGRAPHED IN PATERSON, NEW JERSEY BY NICOLE CIARAMELLA.

OPPOSITE METAL AND LEATHER DETAILS TURN HEATH WALLER'S CONSERVATIVE SUIT INTO SOMETHING DECIDEDLY MORE EDGY. STEAMPUNK COSTUMERS ADD PUNK ELEMENTS TO VICTORIAN-INSPIRED CLOTHES TO ENVISION A WORLD THAT COMBINES THE DISTANT PAST WITH THE POSSIBILITIES OF THE FUTURE. PHOTOGRAPHED BY PAT LYTTLE.

RIGHT JAPANESE ILLUSTRATOR SAKIZOU IS FAMOUS FOR ELEGANT COSTUME DESIGNS. THIS COSPLAY IS BASED ON AN ORIGINAL SAKIZOU ILLUSTRATION THAT BLENDS THE FASHIONS AND FABRIC CHOICES OF VERSAILLES AND TODAY. PHOTOGRAPHED BY MARTIN WONG.

The publishers would like to thank the following sources for their kind permission to reproduce the pictures in this book.

Key: t=Top, b=Bottom, l=Left and r=Right.

Page **2** Joseph Chi Lin; **3** Joseph Chi Lin; **4l** Michael Ooi Photography; **4r** © Nicole Ciarmella; **5l** © Martin Wong; **5c** © Judith Stephens; **5r** © Judith Stephens; **7** Michael Stewart/WireImage/Getty Images; **9** Private Collection; **10** Eleventhphotograph.com; **11** Joseph Chi Lin; **12** Joseph Chi Lin; **14** Tolga Akmen/Anadolu Agenc/Getty Images; **15-16** Tolga Akmen/Anadolu Agenc/Getty Images; **19** © Michael Ooi Photography; **22** Black Rabbit Photography/Thomas Kuan; **23** Black Rabbit Photography/Thomas Kuan; **24** © Michael Ooi Photography; **25t** © Michael Ooi Photography; **25b** © Michael Ooi Photography; **26t** © Michael Ooi Photography; **26b** © Michael Ooi Photography; **27** Black Rabbit Photography/Thomas Kuan; **28** © Judith Stephens; **29** © Judith Stephens; **30** © Martin Wong; **31** © Mineralblu Photography; **32** Black Rabbit Photography/Thomas Kuan; **33l** © Pugoffka; **33r** © Nicole Ciarmella; **34** © Pugoffka; **35** © Pugoffka; **36** Black Rabbit Photography/Thomas Kuan; **37** © Joseph Chi Lin; **38-39** © Big White Bazooka Photography/big Big White Bazooka Photography/bazooka.com; **40** Eleventhphotograph.com; **41** © Pugoffka; **42t** © Nicole Ciaramella; **42b** Eleventhphotograph.com; **43** © Jason Tablante; **44** © Joseph Chi Lin; **45** © Altug Isler; **46** © Benny Lee; **47** © Benny Lee; **48** © Pugoffka; **49** © Pugoffka; **50l** Eleventhphotograph.com; **50-51** © Pugoffka; **52** © Nicole Ciaramella; **53** © Nicole Ciaramella; **54** Eleventhphotograph.com; **55** Eleventhphotograph.com; **56** © Benny Lee; **57** © Michael Ooi Photography; **58-59** © Big White Bazooka Photography/bigwhitebazooka.com; **59r** Guy Bell/Rex Features; **60-61** © Big White Bazooka Photography/bigwhitebazooka.com; **62** © Michael Ooi Photography; **63** © Pugoffka; **64** © Michael Ooi Photography; **65** © Judith Stephens; **66** © Pugoffka; **67l** © Anna Fischer; **67r** © Big White Bazooka Photography/bigwhitebazooka.com; **69** © Nicole Ciaramella; **72** Albert L. Ortega/Getty Images; **73** © Benny Lee; **74-75** Guy Bell/Rex Features; **76t** Guy Bell/Rex Features; **76b** Guy Bell/Rex Features; **77** Guy Bell/Rex Features; **78** Guy Bell/Rex Features; **79** Guy Bell/Rex Features; **80l** Neilson Barnard/Getty Images; **80-81** © Judith Stephens; **82** Guy Bell/Rex Features; **83** Neilson Barnard/Getty Images; **84-85** © Nicole Ciaramella; **86** Neilson Barnard/Getty Images; **87** Neilson Barnard/Getty Images; **88** Neilson Barnard/Getty Images; **89** Guy Bell/Rex Features; **90** Neilson Barnard/Getty Images; **91** © Mineralblu Photography; **92** © Judith Stephens; **93** © Judith Stephens; **94** © Anna Fischer; **95** © Jason Tablante; **96** © Mineralblu Photography; **97** © Jason Tablante; **98l** Guy Bell/Rex Features; **98r** Guy Bell/Rex Features; **99** © Joseph Chi Lin; **100** Guy Bell/Rex Features; **101** © Nicole Ciaramella; **102** © Nicole Ciaramella; **103** © Nicole Ciaramella; **104** © Mineralblu Photography; **105** © Jason Tablante; **106** © Martin Wong; **107** © Judith Stephens; **108** © Anna Fischer; **110** Eleventhphotograph.com; **111** Guy Bell/Rex Features; **112** © Pugoffka; **113** © Pugoffka; **114** © Matthew Chattle/Alamy; **115** Daniel Boczarski/Getty Images; **116** Guy Bell/Rex Features; **117** Guy Bell/Rex Features; **118** Guy Bell/Rex Features; **119** Neilson Barnard/Getty Images; **121** © Martin Wong; **124** Guy Bell/Rex Features; **125** © Jason Tablante; **126** © Martin Wong; **127** © Martin Wong; **128** © Martin Wong; **129t** © Mineralblu Photography; **129b** © Martin Wong; **130** © Nicole Ciaramella; **131** © Nicole Ciaramella; **132** © Pugoffka; **133t** © Nicole Ciaramella; **133b** © Nicole Ciaramella; **134** © Michael Ooi Photography; **135** Black Rabbit Photography/Thomas Kuan; **136t** © Mineralblu Photography; **136b** Guy Bell/Rex Features; **137** © Martin Wong; **138** Eleventhphotograph.com; **139** Eleventhphotograph.com; **140** © Altug Isler; **141** © Altug Isler; **142t** © Nicole Ciaramella; **142b** Eleventhphotograph.com; **143** © Anna Fischer; **144-145** © Benny Lee; **146** © Nicole Ciaramella; **147t** © Big White Bazooka Photography/bigwhitebazooka.com; **147b** © Joseph Chi Lin; **148** © Joseph Chi Lin; **149** © Anna Fischer; **150** Eleventhphotograph.com; **151** © Nicole Ciaramella; **152-153** © Judith Stephens; **153r** Guy Bell/Rex Features; **154-155** © Michael Ooi Photography; **156** © Michael Ooi Photography; **157** © Michael Ooi Photography; **158-159** © Pugoffka; **160-161** © Benny Lee; **161r** © Pugoffka; **162l** © Nicole Ciaramella; **162-163** © Martin Wong; **164** © Judith Stephens; **165** © Anna Fischer; **166** Black Rabbit Photography/Thomas Kuan; **167** © Benny Lee; **168** © Pugoffka; **169** © Big White Bazooka Photography/bigwhitebazooka.com; **170** Black Rabbit Photography/Thomas Kuan; **172** © Judith Stephens; **173** © Judith Stephens; **174-175** © Nicole Ciaramella; **177** © Judith Stephens; **180** Black Rabbit Photography/Thomas Kuan; **181** © Judith Stephens; **182** © Nicole Ciaramella; **183** © Benny Lee; **184** Guy Bell/Rex Features; **185** Guy Bell/Rex Features; **186-187** © Pugoffka; **188-189** © Pugoffka; **190** Eleventhphotograph.com; **191** © Pugoffka; **192** © Judith Stephens; **193** Eleventhphotograph.com; **194-195** © Benny Lee; **196** © Anna Fischer; **197** Black Rabbit Photography/Thomas Kuan; **198-199** © Benny Lee; **200** Guy Bell/Rex Features; **201** © Altug Isler; **202** © Nicole Ciaramella; **203** Tolga Akmen/Anadolu Agency/Getty Images; **204-205** Neilson Barnard/Getty Images; **206** © Mineralblu Photography; **207** Guy Bell/Rex Features; **208** © Nicole Ciaramella; **209** Neilson Barnard/Getty Images; **210** © Joseph Chi Lin; **211** © Pugoffka; **212** © Nicole Ciaramella; **213** Daniel Boczarski/Getty Images; **214-215** Neilson Barnard/Getty Images; **216** Albert L. Ortega/Getty Images; **217** Neilson Barnard/Getty Images; **218-219** Neilson Barnard/Getty Images; **220** Dan Kitwood/Getty Images; **221** © Mineralblu Photography; **222** © Judith Stephens; **223** © Anna Fischer; **224-225** © Martin Wong; **227** © Judith Stephens; **230** © Nicole Ciaramella; **231** © Judith Stephens; **232-233** © Nicole Ciaramella; **234** © Nicole Ciaramella; **235t** © Nicole Ciaramella; **235b** © Nicole Ciaramella; **236** © Nicole Ciaramella; **237** © Nicole Ciaramella; **238** © Nicole Ciaramella; **239** © Nicole Ciaramella; **240-241** © Tommy Bruce; **242** © Tommy Bruce; **243** © Tommy Bruce; **244** Black Rabbit Photography/Thomas Kuan; **245** Black Rabbit Photography/Thomas Kuan; **246-247** © Judith Stephens; **248** © Pugoffka; **249** © Pugoffka; **250** © Nicole Ciaramella; **251** Black Rabbit Photography/Thomas Kuan; **252** Pat Lyttle/Getty Images; **253** © Martin Wong; **254-255** Eleventhphotograph.com

Every effort has been made to acknowledge correctly and contact the source and/or copyright holder of each picture and Carlton Books Limited apologises for any unintentional errors or omissions, which will be corrected in future editions of this book.